D0194792

MARK'S WITNESS TO JESUS CHRIST

WORLD
CHRISTIAN
BOOKS

MARK'S WITNESS TO JESUS CHRIST

by EDUARD LOHSE, Th.D.
of the Johannes-Gutenberg University, Mainz

ASSOCIATION PRESS, NEW YORK

MARK'S WITNESS TO JESUS CHRIST

Association Press, 291 Broadway, New York 7, N. Y.

The series *World Christian Books* is sponsored by the International Missionary Council in co-operation with the Christian Literature Council of Great Britain and the Committee on World Literacy and Christian Literature of the United States. This volume, translated from the German by Bishop Stephen Neill, is published in Great Britain, under the same title, by the United Society for Christian Literature (Lutterworth Press, London), 1955. The Scripture quotations in this book are from the Revised Standard Version of the Bible.

Price, $1.25

Library of Congress catalog card number: 55-7567

 55

Printed in the United States of America
American Book–Stratford Press, Inc., New York

ABOUT WORLD CHRISTIAN BOOKS

TODAY it is not enough to believe; it is necessary also to understand. From every part of the world comes the demand for books that will help the Christian to understand his faith, to find the answers to the questions that he and other men are asking, and to know how to present the faith to others. The series WORLD CHRISTIAN BOOKS is planned to help in this particular area of Christian need. The books are directed in the first place to the "younger churches," but the old distinction between younger and older churches no longer really holds. All churches are faced by the same problems. In all countries the same questions are being asked. The series is specially planned for those who are called to preach and teach, in the hope that the materials given in these books may help them to carry out their task more effectively. But the aim has also been to write so simply that ordinary members of the church who wish to study their faith may be able to use these books as individuals or in study groups and so to grow in knowledge and understanding.

The books are being published first in English, but it is intended that as soon as possible they should be made available in the main languages of the Christian world. Writers have been chosen from various countries and various branches of the church, with special emphasis on the younger churches. This means that there will be a variety of voices, but the aim and the hope is that through many minds and many tongues the faith of the church in its one Lord may be clearly set forth.

STEPHEN NEILL
General Editor

How to Use This Book

IT IS VERY DIFFICULT for Christians to study a Gospel. We know the Gospels too well, or think we do; in consequence it is all too easy to end by not really knowing the Gospels at all. All Christians have a general knowledge of the gospel story; but most of them would find it difficult to say what is in each of the Gospels, and why each Gospel came to be written in just the form in which we find it in the New Testament. Just because we have a general knowledge of the text, and have heard the Gospels read so often in church, it is not easy for us to come to a Gospel with fresh minds and open eyes, and to find out what its message for us really is. This book is written to help us to read one Gospel afresh, and to learn much about it that may not be familiar to us.

The book can be read through in a day or two; but it will not yield much profit to us, unless we are prepared to take a good deal more trouble than a single rapid reading. Here is the way in which the ideal student would tackle the study of this book:

On two successive days, or at intervals of not more than a week, read the Gospel straight through without stopping. This can be done in a single morning, even if the reader takes his time and does not hurry.

Then write down from memory, and without looking at the Bible, what you can remember of the contents of the Gospel.

Open the Bible, and check through what you have written; note carefully what you have omitted, what you have added which is really found only in other Gospels, at what points you have changed the order of events as found in the Gospel.

Next work through Dr. Lohse's book slowly, with the New Testament open beside you. Every reference must be carefully looked up in the Bible.

Re-read the Gospel once again, and consider whether Dr. Lohse has dealt fairly with every part of it. Dr. Lohse's main point is that the Gospel is written from faith to faith; by a man who believes in order to help others to believe in Jesus Christ. But to believe in him as what?

We are challenged to believe in him:

as Jesus, a man who was born and lived at a certain time and place in history;

as the Christ, the one who fulfilled all the hopes of the Jewish people;

as the Messenger, in whom the kingdom of God came upon earth;

as the obedient Servant, who was crucified on behalf of all men;

as the risen Lord, who is always present with His Church;

as the coming King, whose coming the church eagerly awaits.

Finally consider the consequences for us if we accept the challenge to faith which is presented in this Gospel. We shall find that what is demanded of us is:

obedience, even at the cost of death, as Jesus the Son was obedient to the Father; like St. Mark and his first readers, we too live in a hostile world, in which it can never be easy to follow Christ and serve him;

absolute loyalty to the fellowship of the church, through which alone the gospel message has come down to us, and through which Christ continues his work on earth today;

acceptance of responsibility for the proclamation of this gospel, since Christ died for all men, and this good news must be preached to all men everywhere.

The result of our study should be not only a better understanding of who Jesus was, and of what he said and did; but more effective service as Christians, called to live and witness in the world today.

S. N.

Contents

Chapter **1**

The Gospel of Jesus Christ

The Preaching of the Cross and Resurrection of Jesus Christ

THE Gospel of Mark opens with the words: "The beginning of the gospel of Jesus Christ." Clearly these words indicate both the title and the subject of the book. But what does it mean, when the word "gospel" is used in this connection? Usually we understand by the word a written book, like that of Mark. But in the earliest days of the church, in which Mark was living, something rather different was conveyed by the word.

If we wish to grasp exactly what the word "gospel" meant at that time, we must take a glance back to the Old Testament. In the period of the exile of the Jewish people in Babylon (sixth century B.C.), a prophet promised to the afflicted people the consolation of God. The enslaved people will be set free, and God will visibly establish his royal rule. The prophet sees already how that will come about. The exiles are returning home from Babylon. In Jerusalem the people are standing on the towers, awaiting the return of the exiles. Then a herald is seen, speeding before the people on the way to the holy city. He appears on the tops of the mountains and proclaims peace. He brings good news, he proclaims salvation, as he says to Zion: "Your God reigns" (Isaiah 52:7). This is the content of the glad tidings, the gospel: God's rule as king is made manifest; the deliverance of his people draws nigh. So also in the Psalms—the people are called to offer praise to God: "O sing to the Lord a new song; sing to the Lord, all the earth!" (Psalm 96:1). "Say among the nations, 'The Lord reigns!' " (Psalm 96:10). And the prophet speaks of a messenger of good news who is to come, and who will accomplish His work with the full authority of God: "The Spirit of the Lord God is upon me, because the Lord has anointed me to bring good tidings to the afflicted; he has sent me to bind up the brokenhearted, to proclaim liberty to the captives, and the opening of the prison to those who are bound; to proclaim the year of the Lord's favor" (Isaiah 61:1–2).

This messenger of good news, who proclaims the salvation of God, is Jesus—so we are told in the New Testament. In the synagogue at Nazareth, he reads the words of the prophet that have been quoted above, and adds just one word to them: "Today this scripture has been fulfilled in your hearing" (Luke 4:21). And when John the Baptist asks him from prison the question "Are you he who is to come?" Jesus answers with the words: "The blind receive their sight and the lame walk, lepers are cleansed and the deaf hear, and the dead are raised up, and the poor have good news preached to them" (Matthew 11:5). This means that Jesus is that messenger of good news of whom the word of the prophet had spoken. In Him the promises have become a present reality.

In all the passages which we have quoted, the Greek word for the proclamation of the good news is "to proclaim the *evangelion*," the gospel. We see, then, that the meaning of the word "gospel" is "good news." We may add that whenever Christians use the word *evangelion,* they always mean by it the good news of Jesus Christ. For in him the prophecies of the Old Testament have been fulfilled.

It is in this sense that St. Paul also uses the word *evangelion,* which is frequently to be found in his Epistles. The missionaries carry the good news to every part of the world (1 Corinthians 9:12, 16–18, 23). The content of this good news is simply Jesus Christ and nothing else. Paul is aware that this task of proclamation has been laid on him no less than on the other apostles. He expresses this thought most clearly in the Epistle to the Galatians (Galatians 1:11; 2:2, 5, 7, etc.), and in the introduction to the Epistle to the Romans. He has been called to be an apostle, set apart for the gospel of God, "which he promised beforehand through his prophets in the holy scriptures, the gospel concerning his Son, who was descended from David according to the flesh and designated Son of God in power according to the Spirit of holiness by his resurrection from the dead, Jesus Christ our Lord" (Romans 1:2–4). It is probable that, in these verses, Paul is not using his own words, but is taking over phrases in which the early church was already accustomed to express briefly and clearly its faith in Jesus Christ. The *evangelion* is that proclamation of Jesus Christ as Lord, which must be announced to all the world.

These are the terms in which Paul has announced the good news to the churches that he has founded. In an important passage of the First Epistle to the Corinthians, he reminds the Church in solemn words of the gospel message which as their missionary he had brought to them (1 Corinthians 15:1 ff.). He says in plain terms that this was a message which he himself had already received. This message he had then passed on to the Corinthians as that truth through which alone man can attain to salvation. On this affirmation follow three verses which once again probably make use of an existing confession of the faith of the early church, in which the content of the gospel is set forth in a few words: " . . . that Christ died for our sins in accordance with the scriptures, that he was buried, that he was raised on the third day in accordance with the scriptures, and that he appeared to Cephas, then to the twelve" (1 Corinthians 15:3–5).

So the cross and the resurrection of Jesus Christ are the very heart of that proclamation of the gospel to which St. Paul refers. Christ died for our sins according to the Scriptures. No exact indication is given as to the Scripture which is here referred to. But perhaps, more than any other, it is on Isaiah 53, the Song of the Suffering Servant, that these verses are based. Jesus is the Servant of the Lord, who has borne our transgressions. The added clause "he was buried" is intended to make clear that he really died, that he drained the cup of suffering to the bitter end (see Isaiah 53:9). But on the third day God raised him up, as the Scripture had foretold. Here the reference is to such passages as Isaiah 53:11–12 and Hosea 6:2. But it is not only single phrases of the Old Testament that are interpreted as referring to Jesus Christ; he is the fulfiller and perfecter of all the promises of the whole Old Testament—according to the Scriptures. God did not allow the career of Jesus to end with the cross; he raised him up on the third day. This saving event is proclaimed by the apostles as witnesses to their Lord; it is for this reason they are specially mentioned in this passage.

The Acts of the Apostles set before us, in a number of examples, the shape of the earliest Christian preaching. Naturally Luke, the author of Acts, has not supplied us with exact reports of speeches and discourses. In a few verses he sets before us the essentials of that early preaching. Thus, for example, in the story of the first Pentecost of the Christian Church, Peter addresses the astonished Jews as follows: "Men of Israel, hear these words: Jesus of Nazareth, a man attested to you by God with mighty works and wonders and signs which God did through him in your midst, as you yourselves know—this Jesus, delivered up according to the definite plan and foreknowledge of God, you crucified and killed by the hands of lawless men. But God raised him up, having loosed the pangs of death, because it was not possible for him to be held by it" (Acts 2:22–24). There follows a long quotation from Psalm 16:8–11, which is interpreted as a prophecy of the resurrection of Jesus Christ. The discourse ends with the repetition of the central truth: "This Jesus God raised up, and of that we all are witnesses" (Acts 2:32). And finally, as the last word of the sermon, an urgent appeal is addressed to the hearers: "Let all the house of Israel therefore know assuredly that God has made him both Lord and Christ, this Jesus whom you crucified" (Acts 2:36).

From these passages in the Acts of the Apostles, we can work out the plan or outline which was regularly followed in the early Christian preaching of the gospel. The sermon begins with Jesus Christ, his cross and resurrection. His disciples are witnesses of these things, and vouch for the truth of the message as it is proclaimed. Then follows the appeal to Scripture, in which the will of God for the salvation of men had been revealed. Finally, the hearers are directly addressed, and urged to believe the message, to turn from the way in which so far they have walked, and to accept Jesus Christ as their Lord. In the Acts, Luke tells us that the preaching of the apostles and evangelists always included these points, and was constructed according to this outline. This is true of Peter's discourse to the people in Jerusalem, when all were amazed at the healing of a lame beggar (Acts 3:12–

26). It is equally true of the sermon which Peter delivered in Caesarea to a non-Jewish audience (Acts 10:34–43). According to Luke's narrative, Paul in the synagogue in Antioch of Pisidia proclaimed the gospel to Jews in exactly the same manner (Acts 13:23–24).

What is involved in this good news is, however, made plain, not only through quotations from the Old Testament, but also by the recital of acts of Jesus in his ministry, through which the glory of the Messiah was made manifest. Thus the story of the passion of the Lord was linked with the story of the signs and wonders that he had wrought upon earth. For example, Peter in his sermon on the day of Pentecost says that Jesus was a man accredited by God through mighty works, signs, and wonders, of which the Jews already have knowledge (Acts 2:22). Upon this follows the reference to the death and resurrection of Jesus. In the speech of Peter at Caesarea, fuller reference is made to the ministry of Jesus: "You know the word which he sent to Israel, preaching good news of peace by Jesus Christ (he is Lord of all), the word which was proclaimed throughout all Judea, beginning from Galilee after the baptism which John preached: how God anointed Jesus of Nazareth with the Holy Spirit and with power; how he went about doing good and healing all that were oppressed by the devil, for God was with him. And we are witnesses to all that he did both in the country of the Jews and in Jerusalem. They put him to death by hanging him on a tree; but God raised him on the third day" (Acts 10:36–40). Here the preaching of the gospel begins by mentioning John the Baptist, refers to the baptism of Jesus, recounts his mighty works of healing the sick and driving out demons, and comes finally to the cross and resurrection of Jesus. So the arch of the gospel proclamation stretches from the first appearance of John the Baptist to the events of Easter Day.

These examples of early Christian preaching make clear to us that here we have the framework, of which the writers of the Gospels made use, when they faced the task of setting down in writing the essentials of the gospel story. Mark begins with John the Baptist, his preaching of repentance and the baptism that he taught. On this follows the record of the ministry of Jesus—miracles and healings, deeds and words. Finally, we are given, in much fuller detail, the story of the passion and resurrection of the Lord. It is quite clear that Mark regarded this as by far the most important part of what he had to communicate. For here he describes in detail the whole course of the week of the passion in Jerusalem up to the death of Jesus on the cross of Golgotha. In this, Mark is following the preaching of the apostles and evangelists, who had proclaimed the death and resurrection of Jesus as the heart of the gospel, and had carried their message into every part of the world. It is for this reason that Mark begins his Gospel with the words: "The beginning of the gospel of Jesus Christ." This means that this book will be concerned to set forth the content of that good news which the Christian Church exists to proclaim.

Since the heart of the gospel is the cross and resurrection of Jesus, there can be only one gospel. Any other kind of preaching must be accounted false preaching (see Galatians 1:6–9). Only one gospel—and yet we have in the New Testament four books which we are accustomed to call *Gospels*. What is the relationship between these two terms? In the ancient church, the four books which stand at the beginning of the New Testament bore the titles: "The Gospel *according to* Matthew"; "The Gospel *according to* Mark"; "The Gospel *according to* Luke"; "The Gospel *according to* John." The use of this form of speech makes it clear that there is and can be only one gospel. What each of the four Evangelists has composed can be only an *exposition* of this one gospel. All of them, each in his own way, desired to serve the same purpose—through their books to proclaim the good news. As early as the second century A.D., these books which gave an account of the acts and the preaching of Jesus Christ came to be commonly called *Gospels*. Thus it has come about that today we generally speak of four Gospels in the New Testament. But, when we do so, we must not forget that the *gospel* is the good news concerning Jesus Christ, which has been set down by four witnesses in four books. Martin Luther, therefore, was quite right when he said: "Gospel means nothing other than the preaching and proclamation of the grace and mercy of God, obtained and won for us by the Lord Christ through His death. Properly, it is not that which is contained in books and letters, but rather an oral preaching and a living word, a voice which rings out in all the world, and cries out in public so that everywhere it is heard."

The Tradition of the Words and Deeds of Jesus

We have seen that the cross and resurrection of Jesus Christ together make up the content of that which can properly be called the gospel. In consequence, at a very early date, a narrative of these events, such as we find in the passion-story as given by Mark, had already come into existence. But we must ask further what had happened with regard to the tradition of the deeds and words of Jesus. What account was given of his activity in Galilee, Judea, and Jerusalem?

From the Epistles of the apostles, we can gather that, in the oral preaching and instruction given in the church, single utterances of Jesus or stories concerning him were told or quoted by way of example. When the Christians in Thessalonica were distressed because some of their number had died before the second coming of Christ, which they expected would take place in the very near future, Paul comforted them with a saying of Jesus which had been handed down orally in Christian circles (1 Thessalonians 4:15–17). At that time, written Gospels did not yet exist (about A.D. 49–50). And the saying of the Lord to which Paul refers is not found in exactly this form in any of our Gospels. But, in the phrases which Paul quotes as an utterance of Jesus, the question of the Thessalonians is answered: on the day of the second coming of Jesus, those who have fallen asleep will be raised up, so that the fellowship of Christians who are still alive will be reunited with those who have been raised up from the dead to welcome the Lord on his return from heaven. In other places in his Epistles, Paul refers to relevant words of the Lord, which he passes on to his readers. These words of the Lord are always treated with special reverence, since in all that concerns the life of the Christian they possess unconditional authority. For instance, in 1 Corinthians 7, Paul deals with questions of marriage and of the unmarried state. When he is addressing married members of the Christian community, he says: "To the married I give charge, not I but the Lord, that the wife should not separate from her husband" (1 Corinthians 7:10). This saying of Jesus is familiar to us from Matthew 5:32 and Mark 10:11–12. Since Jesus has laid down with such emphatic clearness the principle that a marriage, once made, cannot be dissolved, on this subject there is for Christians a command which has binding authority. But this is not the case with questions on which it was not possible to quote a clear decision of the Lord. In such cases, Paul says that he reaches a decision by the use of his own ability (1 Corinthians 7:12). In another connection, Paul can once again quote a saying of the Lord to the effect that it is the duty of the Christian fellowship to support the preacher of the gospel (1 Corinthians

9:14). We have the word of the Lord that "the laborer deserves his wages" (Luke 10:7). This question, then, is decided beyond dispute; since these words of Jesus which have been handed down in the traditions of the Christian community have binding authority. In 1 Corinthians 11:23–25, we find not a single saying but a whole section in which Paul quotes the early Christian tradition of the Last Supper of Jesus with his disciples. This example makes it clear that single stories of the life of Jesus, as well as sayings, were at first handed on by word of mouth. They were repeated as illustrations in the course of preaching, or cited as rules of conduct for the guidance of Christians in their daily life. It was only later that the single stories and traditions were brought together into connected narratives, and finally into complete Gospels.

If we wish to form a picture of the way in which the tradition of the acts and words of Jesus was formed, we can make use of the examples we have already found in the Epistles in the New Testament. Short sayings of Jesus, like that on the prohibition of divorce, or the teaching that a laborer is worthy of his hire, were so impressive that they could easily be retained in the memory and repeated. And the parables which Jesus had uttered were so graphic that here, too, there was no difficulty in their being passed on from mouth to mouth.

The sayings and parables of Jesus at first existed only in Aramaic, the language that he had spoken, but it was not long before they were translated into Greek. Greek was at that time the universal language, which was understood by the majority of the inhabitants of the Roman Empire. This work of translation must have been done at a very early period, since Paul is able to quote the sayings of Jesus in Greek.

As these sayings passed from mouth to mouth in the process of oral tradition, inevitably additions, expansions, and explanations tended to gather round them. Men were influenced by the desire to pass on the words of Jesus in such a form that they would be directly relevant to the immediate present.* For instance, in 4:3–9 we are given the parable of the sower. This is followed by an explanation, in which the meaning of the parable is set forth in such a way as to remind the hearer of the Christian preaching directly and in warning tones of his responsibility (4:13–20). It is likely that this explanation in its present form goes back, not directly to the words of Jesus himself, but to the thoughts of that early Christian Church, within which the tradition of the words of Jesus was developed. We shall return later to this question. In other contexts also we may be inclined to feel that the form in which the words of Jesus are reproduced has been influenced by their use in Christian preaching. For instance, the three prophecies of his passion which Jesus made to his disciples have been written down in such a form that they look like short summaries of the history of the passion, and mention each of the stages on the way of Jesus to the cross: "Behold, we are going up to Jerusalem, and the Son of man will be delivered to the chief priests and the scribes, and they will condemn him to death, and deliver him to the Gentiles; and they will mock him, and spit upon him, and scourge him, and kill him, and after three days he will rise" (8:31; 9:31; 10:32–34). It is at once clear that these sayings correspond very closely to the gospel-message of the early church concerning the cross and the resurrection. They clearly express the truth that the proclamation of the earthly ministry of Jesus and the preaching of the death and resurrection of the Christ belong together and form

* From this point on, only chapter and verse are given for quotations from St. Mark's Gospel; for all other biblical references, the book of the Bible also is given.

a unity. Therefore, it is impossible to accept the sayings of Jesus, and at the same time to wish to know nothing of his cross and resurrection. On the contrary, the message of Jesus, all that he said, can be understood only by those who accept the gospel as it was preached by the church. It is only through the preaching of the apostolic church that we make contact with the words of Jesus. When this is remembered, we shall not as Christians be shocked to find that the apostles and evangelists added explanations to the words which Jesus had spoken. For the record concerning Jesus which we find in the books that we call Gospels does not set out to be a biographical narrative; its aim is to call Christian faith into being.

Like the words and discourses of Jesus, the stories of his acts were at first passed on from mouth to mouth in oral tradition. The essentials of the story were set forth in short concise phrases; so much so, that in many cases the record of the most important events is compressed into a few verses. The account of the Last Supper of Jesus, which St. Paul has recorded for us in 1 Corinthians 11:23–26, takes up only four verses. St. Paul lays stress on the fact that this is a tradition which he has already received from others. It is clear that the account of the Last Supper had reached a fixed and definite form in the very earliest days of the life of the Christian Church; since, if we compare the phrases used by St. Paul with the words of the Evangelists, who wrote considerably later than St. Paul, we can see that there is close agreement between them. Since this story was of such immense importance in the life of the church, it was constantly repeated, and generally the same words and phrases came to be used. From our written records we can work back to the earliest form of the narrative concerning the Lord's Supper, as it was current in the church in the years immediately following the Lord's death.

In the same way that St. Paul introduces the story of the Last Supper into his letter to the Corinthians, other Christian preachers introduced other stories from the ministry of Jesus as illustrations of their sermons. For instance, we read in St. Mark's Gospel of a dispute between Jesus and the Pharisees about the authority of the law concerning the Sabbath day (2:23–28); the decisive word of Jesus on the subject spoke directly to the problems which the Christian Church was facing at the time when the Gospel was written: "The sabbath was made for man, not man for the sabbath; so the Son of man is lord even of the sabbath." In another passage, we read that the disciples tried to keep away children who were being brought to Jesus. He was indignant at this, and said: " 'Let the children come to me, do not hinder them; for to such belongs the kingdom of God. Truly, I say to you, whoever does not receive the kingdom of God like a child shall not enter it.' And he took them in his arms and blessed them, laying his hands upon them" (10:13–16). Here the scene is drawn in brief, sharp phrases; everything that is not essential is reduced to the narrowest limits, in order to allow the words and acts of Jesus and nothing else to fill the picture. Certainly this incident must often have been quoted as an example, and apparently even in early times it was used to justify the practice of baptizing infants as well as adults.

In other places, however, we find events narrated at much greater length. Details are given about the sickness with which a man was afflicted, about his state of mind and his sufferings. The events leading up to the healing are carefully recorded, and attention is drawn to the greatness of the miracle. For instance, no less than twenty verses are taken up with the description of the healing of a man possessed with devils in Gerasa. But in this account there is no clearly decisive word of the Lord. Here we feel that the chief interest of those who handed on this story was just in telling a story; and this narrative is in some ways like stories of miracles that we find elsewhere in popular and non-Christian sources. We have to reckon with the possibility that the *form* in which this story has come down to us has been affected by non-Christian influences. In such stories we do not feel that we are so close to Jesus as in those short narratives in which the words and deeds of Jesus are clearly set forth, and their importance for the life of the Christian fellowship is made plain.

In the Christian tradition concerning Jesus, a large number of single sayings, parables, and stories circulated, as they were passed on from mouth to mouth. But nothing was said as to the *period* in the ministry of Jesus—whether the beginning or the end—to which each belonged. In such questions these early Christians were not much interested. They were not able to say for certain whether it was at the beginning of his activity or near its end that Jesus had cleansed the temple of traders and shopkeepers (cf. John 2:13–17 with Mark 11:15–19). What they were interested in was bearing witness to the fact that by this action he had revealed himself as Messiah and Lord. The tradition did not make it clear whether he had begun to have conflicts with the scribes and Pharisees even in the early days of his ministry (2—3), or whether these belonged rather to its end (11—12). No special interest was taken in supplying definite information with regard to places and dates. What was all-important was that the Lord had proclaimed the good news to the poor, and had defended them against the respectable folk who had objected to his doing so. No one in that early Christian world considered it an important occupation to draw up a cool, detached record of the life of Christ, in which every event should be carefully entered, but in which the narrator stood outside the events that he was narrating. On the contrary, it was their view that everything that was related about Jesus must directly serve the Christian task of proclaiming the good news.

As we have seen, in that earliest period of Christian life, single sayings and stories of Jesus were related and passed on. But it was not long before, even in that oral tradition, certain connections were made, and a number of separate sayings and incidents were brought together in continuous narrative. One method which was often used to impress on the memory a group of sayings was arrangement according to "catchwords." That is to say, that to one saying which contained a certain word was attached another saying containing the same word, though as regards subject the second might have little or nothing to do with the first. This is the way in which the chain of sayings to be found in 9:33–50, for example, has been built up. We can follow the catchwords "child" (36–37), "in my name" (37–38), "cause to sin" (42, 43, 45, 47), "fire" (48, 49), "salt" (49, 50).

In a number of other cases, it was similarity of form or subject that provided the occasion for bringing together a number of separate sections into a continuous whole. Thus we find not only one parable of Jesus related, but several parables together. Or several miracles are narrated one after the other, thus giving rise to a whole series of such stories (4:35—5:43). Or it may be a series of disputes between Jesus and the scribes and Pharisees which are brought together as a single whole (11:27—12:40). Elsewhere, a whole long section of traditional material is made up of the conflicts between Jesus and those who were opposed to his preaching. These stories are told one after the other without interruption; but it does not necessarily follow that they all occurred in equally close connection with one another in the life and ministry of Jesus. It is much more likely that because they dealt with much the same subject, such single episodes were brought together in the development of the oral tradition concerning Jesus.

We can thus discern a clearly marked process in the formation of this oral tradition. First, single sayings, utterances, and acts of Jesus were recited, referred to in preaching, used in the instruction of the Christian people, and passed on from mouth to mouth. Then the single stories were brought together in sequences, clearly defined by the subjects with which they dealt. In this way, longer sections of the story of Jesus were brought into existence. Mark took over these longer sections from the traditions of the church and from its preaching, and used them as the material out of which he built up his book.

chapter 2

How Mark's Gospel Came to Be Written

The Structure of the Book

THE task which Mark had set before himself was to bring together in one single book the separate stories and connected sections of the life of Jesus that had been circulating in the oral tradition. For many parts of his material, the point at which each should be included in his book was fixed in advance by the subject with which it dealt. There could be no doubt that the story of John the Baptist must come at the beginning, and that the stories of the passion and of the resurrection must come at the end of the book. Jesus had exercised his ministry in Galilee, in Judea, and in Jerusalem. In the case of some stories the tradition had made it clear where the event referred to had taken place. Obviously the cleansing of the temple could only have happened in Jerusalem. Of other events it was equally clear that they must have happened in Galilee—for instance, everything which occurred in or near Capernaum (1:21 ff.). On the other hand, of many events it was no longer possible to say exactly when and where they had taken place. An instance is the dispute of Jesus with the scribes and Pharisees about the ritual washing of hands (7:1–23); no indication is given of the stage of the ministry of Jesus at which this took place. We look in vain in the traditions concerning the life of Jesus for data from which it is possible to draw exact conclusions as to the year or the month in which particular events took place.

Thus the Evangelist had no easy task in bringing together into a unity the many and various fragments of tradition that had come down to him. Since the aim that he had set before himself was the drawing up of a "Gospel of Jesus Christ," he took over the outline with which he was already familiar from the Christian preaching of the early days. Into this outline, which stretched from the preaching of John the Baptist to the resurrection of Jesus, Mark introduced the stories concerning Jesus that had come to his knowledge, linking them loosely together. Each story was provided with a short introduction and conclusion, and in this way a more or less continuous narrative, a more or less unified picture was produced. In many cases it is no more than the little word "and" which links one story to that which has preceded it (1:14, 16, 21, etc.). In some cases, Mark introduces brief notes, which serve as a bridge from one story to another. In 3:9, we read of the order given by Jesus to his disciples to have a boat ready for him. This point is taken up again in 4:1, where we find Jesus, in Mark's account, sitting in the boat and teaching the crowd in parables. When he has finished his teaching in parables, the boat appears again; Jesus enters the boat, and sets off with his disciples on the journey across the lake of Galilee (4:36). The boat carries them to the other side of the lake, where Jesus heals a man possessed by evil spirits. By this simple means, Mark has made a connection between a number of very different elements in the tradition which had come down to him. But the connection between them has not been very closely drawn, and from this we can infer that it is Mark himself who has made the connection. For, if we were set to work to find in this passage exact indications of the course followed by the life of Jesus or the period covered by his ministry, we should find that our calculations could lead to no certain conclusions. If we started from 3:9, and from our Lord's command that a boat should be ready for him, we might be led to think that all the other events in connection with which this little vessel is referred to had taken place on the same day. This is not absolutely impossible; but surely it is not very likely. First we find stories of healings and miracles (3:10–11). Then follows the call of the twelve disciples (3:13–19), with which a controversy with the Pharisees is closely connected (3:20–35). Next Jesus calls for the boat, and sitting in it delivers his long discourse, containing several parables (4:1–34). We may be inclined to think that this is already as many events as a single day will hold. But now Jesus with his disciples makes the journey to the far side of the stormy lake of Gennesaret (4:35—5:1). According to 4:35, this crossing began only in the late afternoon, "when evening had come," and since the distance to be covered was something like five to eight miles, a considerable time must be allowed for this. So, carrying our calculations a little further, we find that Jesus and his disciples would have arrived on the other shore late in the evening. But Mark finds no difficulty in recording the healing of the man of Gerasa, who was possessed by evil spirits, as having taken place immediately upon their arrival (5:1–20). We are not yet at the end. After this, Jesus and his disciples again enter into the boat, and cross the lake once more to the western shore, whereupon two further outstanding miracles are performed (5:21–43). It is hardly possible to suppose that so many events can all have taken place in a single day. It is much more likely that Mark felt no particular concern to let us know over how many days these events were spread. The brief notes at the beginning and end of each section serve the purpose of bringing together in loose connection a number of separate elements in the oral tradition.

Another example will help to show that these connections between the different sections are the work of the Evangelist himself. In 1:16–20, we read of the call of the first disciples of Jesus. When Jesus calls them to follow him, they are actually engaged in their work as fishermen. In Mark's account, the event which follows immediately upon this is that Jesus enters with his disciples into the synagogue at Capernaum on the Sabbath day (1:21–28). But actually these two events cannot possibly have taken place on the same day, since no Jew could carry on any work on the Sabbath day, and certainly not the work of fishing. So, here again, Mark has brought two stories into loose connection with one another, though it is evident that the two events cannot have happened on the same day.

The order, then, of the events which Mark records was drawn up by the Evangelist himself, in fulfillment of his task of creating a unity out of the many and various traditions that he had received. In consequence, much is absent from his book which certainly would have been included in it if his aim had been to write a "life of Jesus," a biography in the ordinary sense of the word. There is no hint of any development in Jesus, as for instance, of his understanding of himself as the Messiah; on the contrary, Jesus is from the beginning the Messiah (1:1), the Son of God (1:11). Again we cannot say that, according to Mark's account, the enmity of the Jews to Jesus gradually developed; it is rather the case that from the beginning the shadow of the cross falls upon the path of Jesus (2:20; 3:6). As early as 3:22 there is a mention of scribes from Jerusalem, who declare war upon Jesus. Thus the book which Mark wrote is determined from beginning to end by one single aim—that of presenting Jesus as the crucified and risen Messiah. All the riches of the material which Mark took over from the early Christian tradition is arranged in accordance with this one guiding principle.

Those longer sections, which had come into existence in the development of the oral tradition, Mark took over exactly as they stood, and fitted them into his outline. So his book contains a number of these longer sections, already formed in the oral tradition, which the Evangelist fitted into his work at what seemed to him the most appropriate point. We shall now attempt to make clear the structure of the book, by taking a rapid journey through the Gospel according to St. Mark.

1. Mark begins with a prologue (1:1–13), which may be compared with the introduction to the Gospel according to St. John (John 1:1–18). John the Baptist appears as the one sent to prepare the way for the Coming One, as had been foretold in the Scriptures of the Old Testament (see Malachi 3:1; Isaiah 40:3). He preaches in the wilderness, and baptizes in the waters of Jordan. He proclaims the coming of One who is stronger than he, who will baptize with the Holy Ghost. Jesus of Nazareth also comes to the Jordan—the Servant of God takes his place in the community of the people of God. Who this Jesus is, is made clear to the reader by the divine voice, which at his baptism designates him as Messiah: "Thou art my beloved Son; with thee I am well pleased" (1:11). After this, Jesus endures the assaults of the tempter (1:

12–13). Long ago the first man in paradise had failed to withstand temptation (Genesis 3), but Jesus remains victor in the fight. "And he was with the wild beasts." Here the prologue ends. With these words the Evangelist reminds us of that garden of Eden from which Adam was driven out. Jesus brings back the uncorrupted world, as God originally made it. Through Adam, sin and death entered into the world (Romans 5:12 ff.); but through the one man, Jesus Christ, God's grace and gifts are made richly available to all (Romans 5:15).

2. In 1:14–45 mark tells us of the first appearance of Jesus in and near Capernaum. He begins his ministry with the call to repentance and faith in the good news. He calls his first disciples, heals a man possessed by evil spirits in the synagogue of Capernaum, and restores Peter's wife's mother to health. He heals many sick people of their diseases, but then withdraws himself from the throngs of men in order to pray alone. The first chapter ends with the healing of a leper. Thus in word and deed Jesus reveals his majesty.

3. In chapters 2 and 3 are included a number of stories dealing with controversies between Jesus and the religious leaders, the scribes and Pharisees. They contest his right to forgive sins. They are offended by his easy friendship with publicans and sinners. They criticize the disciples of Jesus for not fasting. They are indignant that Jesus does not observe the rules laid down in the law about the keeping of the Sabbath day. They accuse Jesus of having made a covenant with the devil, and so obtaining the power to perform His mighty works. The inevitable result of these controversies is that the enemies of Jesus declare open war upon him, and take counsel how to get rid of him (3:6). Jesus, however, continues to heal the sick, and chooses twelve disciples, whom he gathers round

himself, and sends forth to proclaim the good news and to overcome the evil powers (3:7–12, 13–19).

4. In the fourth chapter follows another connected section from the old tradition—the teaching of Jesus in parables (4:1–34). Three parables are given one after the other—the sower, the seed growing secretly, and the mustard seed. But the connection is broken by the introduction, after the first parable (vss. 10 ff.), of a separate section containing a special piece of instruction given by Jesus to his disciples. The secret of the kingdom of God has been given to the disciples, but to those who are without, everything remains mysterious.

5. The boat, which has already been mentioned in 3:9 and 4:1, serves as the bridge to the next group of stories. Here Mark introduces a connected section in which the common subject is the mighty works of Jesus (4:35—5:43). Jesus is Lord over wind and sea; he is Lord over evil spirits, sickness, and death.

6. Next follows a series of detached incidents, in which the subject is again the enmity that was directed toward Jesus. When he preached in the synagogue of his own city Nazareth, his claims were rejected (6:1–6). Herod, the ruler of Galilee, and the prince to whom Jesus as a Galilean was subject, is reminded, by what he hears about the work of Jesus, of John the Baptist, whom he had had put to death (6:14–29). But, just as in the narrative of Chapter 3 Jesus in spite of all the opposition gathers his flock about him, so here also he gives to the disciples the command to go forth and to proclaim the good tidings (6:6–13). When they have fulfilled their task, they return to the Lord in order to report to him on what they have done (6:30–33).

7. Now we pass to another connected section, of which the central theme is the miraculous feeding of the

crowds (6:34—8:26). We have in fact two accounts of such miracles; and some scholars have concluded that these are not two separate miracles, but that Mark has taken from different sources two accounts of the same event, and placed them one after the other in his Gospel. There are only minor differences between the two accounts of the miraculous feeding (6:34–44 and 8:1–9). Further, the other small sections which follow in each case are in a number of ways similar to one another. This may be made clear by the following table:

6:34–44	Feeding of the multitude	8: 1–9
6:45–46	Crossing the lake	8:10
7: 1–15	Controversy	8:11–13
7:17–23	Instructions to the disciples	8:14–21
7:31–37	A narrative of healing	8:22–26

The many differences in the details of the stories make clear that Mark is drawing on different sources. But, whether we have here accounts of two separate miracles, or two different accounts of the same miracle, in either case Mark's principal concern is to set forth Jesus as the giver of the bread of life. To these accounts of the miraculous feeding, Mark has attached a sequence of short sections, which had already found their place in this order in the sources on which he drew.

8. WITH 8:27 BEGINS A NEW SERIES OF CONNECTED STORIES, which can be grouped together under the general title "On the Way to the Cross." The first of these deals with Peter's confession of Jesus as Messiah at Caesarea Philippi. This marks a decisive turning point in Mark's Gospel. After Peter's confession we find a number of sections, drawn from the tradition, in which Jesus is shown as concentrating on the instruction of the disciples. Now the ministry of Jesus is no longer concerned with the mass of the people; instead, he is occupied with mak-

ing clear to the disciples that he must suffer and die, and then rise again. Three times is this prediction repeated (8:31; 9:30–32; 10:32–34). And on each occasion the prediction is followed by instructions to the disciples. Through the account of the transfiguration (9:2–8) Mark makes it clear in advance that Jesus will emerge as victor in the strife. Following the third prediction is the story of the conversation of Jesus with the sons of Zebedee, which ends with a most important utterance: "For the Son of man also came not to be served but to serve, and to give his life as a ransom for many" (10:45). Here is given the interpretation of the death of Jesus: he died to win the forgiveness of our sins, as was stated in the early Christian preaching (1 Corinthians 15:3). In Jericho, Jesus heals a blind man. Thus this section, like that which comes before it (8:22–26), ends with the healing of blindness. Jesus opens the eyes of the blind in order that they may see. But those who can see fail to recognize him!

9. JESUS NOW ARRIVES IN JERUSALEM, and in Chapters 11—13 Mark tells the story of the last days of His life. He enters the holy city as Messiah, greeted with enthusiasm by the crowds. He cleanses the temple of traders and money-changers. But the coming judgment is already suspended over Israel (11:12–14, 20–26). The leaders of the people are so bitterly hostile to Jesus that they are only awaiting their opportunity to destroy him (11:18). The intensity of the conflict is shown in the series of disputes which follow (11:27—12:40). To the question about his authority, Jesus avoids giving an answer. In the parable of the wicked husbandmen (tenants of the vineyard) Jesus makes plain to his enemies what it is that they are preparing to do. Jesus carries on a series of sharp encounters with the Pharisees and Sadducees, and at the end of the section are recorded the stern words which he spoke also against the scribes. After these controversies, Mark re-

cords a discourse which Jesus delivered to the faithful disciples only (13). Here he reveals to them all that will happen in the last times up to the coming of the Son of man. Thus the story of these days, shadowed by the sufferings which Jesus is about to undergo, ends with a forward glance to that final victory of God, which the people of God await with eager expectation.

10. NOW MARK'S ACCOUNT OF THE LIFE OF JESUS HAS REACHED ITS CLIMAX. The conflict has reached the final limit of bitterness. Jesus is betrayed, condemned, and tormented. Silently he endures his suffering as the obedient Servant of God, and dies the most shameful of deaths upon the cross (14—15). But on the third day he is raised again by God. Some women who had gone to his tomb receive from the mouth of an angel the news that he has risen. Trembling and astonishment come upon them at this announcement, for they were greatly afraid (16:1–8).

The Composition of the Book

When was the Gospel of Mark written? The first point that we can make, in attempting to answer this question, is that the Gospel of Mark is the earliest of our four Gospels. In this study, we need not consider in detail the Gospel according to St. John, since that Gospel was written only toward the end of the first century A.D. We have to deal here only with the Gospels of Matthew, Mark, and Luke.

If these three Gospels are written out in sections and placed side by side in the form of a synopsis, it becomes clear that Matthew and Luke knew Mark's Gospel and made use of it. In arranging the material which they have taken over from Mark, they keep the sections in the same order as that in which they are found in Mark. In the stories of the birth of Jesus, on the contrary, which

Matthew and Luke have derived from different sources in the tradition, they differ widely from one another. It is only when they come to the story of John the Baptist, which they recount very much as it lay before them in Mark's Gospel, that they agree closely with one another. The same is true of the concluding sections of the Gospel. Matthew and Luke have both taken over the story as it is recorded in Mark 16:1–8. But from this point, at which Mark ceased to serve them as a model, they begin again to differ very much from one another. This makes it almost certain that Matthew and Luke made use of the Gospel of Mark in the preparation of their own Gospels. And in that case, Mark must have been written before the other two.

We can reach the same conclusion also by comparing what is to be found in each of the three Gospels at various points. Mark tells us that in answer to the question of Jesus as to who the disciples believed him to be, Peter answered simply: "You are the Christ" (8:29). Both Matthew and Luke have recorded this important scene, but seem to have felt that this brief phrase in Mark was too short to express fully the confession of faith in Jesus as the Christ. Therefore, each of them expanded the phrase. Matthew has: "You are the Christ, the Son of the living God" (Matthew 16:16); Luke, rather more briefly: "the Christ of God" (Luke 9:20). What we find in Mark is the oldest and simplest form of Peter's confession; this the other Synoptists (this is the common name given to the three Evangelists, Matthew, Mark, and Luke) later explained in fuller terms. Here is another example of the same process: In Mark 10:35, we read that the two sons of Zebedee, James and John, came to Jesus and asked that they might have the privilege of sitting one on his right hand and one on his left in his glory. It seems that both the other Synoptists felt a difficulty here; was it really the two disciples themselves who made this bold request of their Master? Luke does not refer at all to the request. Matthew, perhaps using another form of the tradition, writes more cautiously that it was the mother of the sons of Zebedee who came and asked that to her sons might be granted the special place of honor (Matthew 20:20–28). This avoids the difficulty of representing James and John themselves as making so selfish and ambitious a request of their Master.

In a number of cases the other two Evangelists make the narrative clearer and more exact. For instance, Mark states that while David was fleeing from Saul, he came to the house of God, when Abiathar was high priest (2:26). A reference to the Old Testament makes it clear that the name of the high priest at that time was Ahimelech, and that he was the father of Abiathar (1 Samuel 21:1–6; 22:20–23). Matthew and Luke have avoided a seeming disagreement with the Old Testament by omitting the name Abiathar in their accounts of this incident (Matthew 12:4; Luke 6:4). Again, Mark refers to Herod, the ruler to whom Jesus was subject, as "king" (6:14). To be quite exact, Herod had not the title of "king," but only that of "tetrarch" (ruler of a quarter of the land); that is to say, he was no more than the ruler of a small district under the authority of the Romans. Matthew and Luke in referring to Herod make use of the more accurate term "tetrarch" (Matthew 14:1; Luke 9:7). Such small changes suggest that Mark is the oldest of our Gospels, and that Matthew and Luke made use of his work in preparing their own Gospels.

Mark writes in a simple, popular style. He writes as people spoke, in the style of the oral traditions and preaching concerning Jesus. He does not employ long, complicated sentences, such as were regarded with favor in the literary style of that time, and such as St. Luke, who had been well educated in the Greek language, was able to construct (e.g., Luke 1:1–4). It seems that Mark is often reproducing exactly the oral tradition and preaching of the church. Nowhere do we receive the impression that he is using earlier written sources. Thus we may say with confidence that Mark wrote the first complete Gospel that ever existed, and that there were not, before his time, other and earlier written Gospels which have since disappeared.

When did Mark write? Nowhere in his Gospel—not even in the predictions concerning the coming catastrophe (13)—is there any hint that judgment has already fallen upon Jerusalem. Now in the year A.D. 70, Jerusalem had been captured by the Romans and entirely destroyed. Mark tells us nothing of these events. It is, therefore, probable that he was writing earlier than A.D. 70.

Who was the author of the book? His name is not mentioned anywhere in it. Evidently the author was not concerned to tell us anything about himself. The messenger is entirely hidden behind the message, which it is his task to deliver. In the traditions of the early church the name of the writer of this Gospel is given as Mark, and we have every reason to regard this tradition as reliable. Mark was not an apostle, but we have a certain amount of information about him. His mother, Mary, is referred to in the Acts of the Apostles. She was an outstanding member of the Church in Jerusalem, and owned a house in which meetings of the first Christians were held (Acts 12:12). Mark went with Barnabas and Paul on their first missionary journey (Acts 12:25; 13:5), but left them in the course of it (Acts 13:13). Later he appears to have been again a companion of St. Paul, since he is mentioned in Philemon 24, Colossians 4:10 and 2 Timothy 4:11 as one of his fellow workers. At the end of the first Epistle of Peter, Mark is found with Peter at Rome (Babylon is probably a secret name for Rome) (1 Peter 5:13). Mark, then, was a native of Jerusalem, and had gone with the apostles in their journeys. He was not himself a disciple of Jesus, but he had received from the apostles the message of Jesus Christ and the stories of his earthly ministry.

To these notices in the New Testament, which we may well take as referring to the author of the second Gospel, we may add a piece of information given us by Papias, Bishop of Hierapolis in the second century A.D. He writes that Mark was the interpreter of Peter, and wrote down what he had gathered from the teaching given by Peter. He did not write down these pieces of instruction in chronological order; Peter had given his instructions as circumstances demanded. Mark had then preserved them in written form as he remembered them. This information fits in well with what we have inferred from the Gospel itself—that Mark gathered his material for it from oral tradition. And Papias may well have been right in saying that a large part of the traditions which Mark used went back to Peter (see, for example, 1:29–39; 8:27–33; 14:53–72).

So much for what we can learn about the writer of our Gospel. We turn finally to the question: "For whom did he write his book?" Who were the readers whom he had in mind while he was writing? Clearly these readers were not Jews but Gentile Christians. They knew only the Greek language in which Mark was writing to them, and were not familiar with Jewish manners and customs; these had to be explained to them (e.g., 7:3–4; 14:12; 15:42). When Mark uses Hebrew or Aramaic expressions, as he does fairly often, he translates them for the benefit of his readers (3:17, Boanerges—sons of thunder; 5:41, Talitha cumi—"Little girl, I say to you, arise"; 7:11, Corban—given to God; 7:34, Ephphatha—be opened; 14:36, Abba—Father; 15:22, Golgotha—the place of a skull; 15:34, Eloi, Eloi, lama sabachthani—My God, my God, why hast thou forsaken me?) These examples make it clear that the intended readers are Gentile Christians, who are not familiar either with the speech or the customs of the Jews. Mark, then, is writing for people who had been far from God, but who had now become believers in Jesus Christ. His book has in mind the world-wide church, which through the preaching of the gospel is everywhere in process of being founded (see 13:10).

Although Mark's Gospel was written in Greek, there are a number of Latin words in it (5:9, Legion; 6:27, a soldier of the guard; 6:37, denarii (denarius—penny); 12:14, taxes; 12:42, penny (in older translations, "farthing"); 15:16, praetorium; 15:39, 44 ff., centurion). In 6:48 and 13:35 we find the night divided into four watches, and these correspond to the system of setting guards followed in the Roman army. In 10:11–12, it is implied that a wife can separate herself from her husband. This was the case in Roman law, under which a wife, no less than a husband, could seek to be free from her marriage. These expressions, however, which reveal the influence of Latin, are limited to words and phrases which had been carried by Roman soldiers to every part of the Roman Empire; and we cannot, therefore, base any definite conclusions on these observations. It is to be noted, however, that in the traditions of the ancient church, Rome is often mentioned as the place at which the Gospel of Mark was written. We can at least say that the instances of Latin influence collected above fit in well with this tradition. If this is so, it is probable that the Gospel was written shortly after the persecution under the emperor Nero, in which many Christians, Peter among them, had lost their lives. Mark wished to fix the apostolic preaching in written form, and so to preserve it for the church.

chapter 3

Jesus the Messiah

The Jewish Expectation of a Messiah

IN the very first verse of his book, Mark speaks of Jesus as the Christ, that is, as the Messiah (Christ in Greek is the same as Messiah in Hebrew; both mean "the anointed one"). When the Christian Church confessed its faith in Jesus as the Messiah, it was applying to Jesus a title which had its origin in Jewish expectations of the time of the end. But what is the meaning implied in this confession of faith in Jesus as the Messiah?

If we wish to answer this question, we must first try to make a brief general survey of the Jewish expectations which looked forward to the coming of the Messiah. This Jewish hope was by no means uniform; it took on a number of different and distinct forms.

The messianic expectation of most of the Jews in the time of Jesus took the form of the hope of the coming of a mighty king, who would deliver the people from subjection and set them free to attain to new greatness. He is called Messiah, the anointed one, because he will receive royal dignity and sovereign authority. He will be a powerful king, such as David was of old. For that reason he is also referred to as David's son, since Messiah is to proceed from the family of David. He will wage war with a mighty arm and overcome the enemy. He will triumph over them, drive them all out of the land of Israel, and purify Jerusalem from the defilements of the heathen. He will bring together the twelve tribes of the people, which are now scattered abroad, and so will gather together the people of God in its entirety in the Holy Land. Then will dawn a period of prosperity, and blessed is he who is counted worthy to share in the happiness of those days. Certainly in the time of Jesus, under the oppressive rule of the Romans and of Herod, this hope was very active, and filled the hearts of many Jews.

Along with this *political* form of the expectation of Messiah, there were other forms of the hope of a deliverer, who was to appear at the end of the days. Thus Deuteronomy 18:15 was interpreted to mean that God's messenger, who would come in the last days, would be a prophet such as Moses had been of old. In that verse it was written: "The Lord your God will raise up for you a prophet like me from among you, from your brethren—him you shall heed." This expectation of the appearance of a prophet in the last days is clearly referred to in several passages of the New Testament (see Mark 8:28; John 1:21; 6:14).

In other circles among the Jews, the opinion was held that the messenger of God in the last days would be a priest of the house of Aaron, who would sanctify the people of God and gather them together in priestly purity, that they might be consecrated to God. He would bind Satan, and deprive the evil spirits of their power, and open the gates of paradise, and give the saints to eat of the fruit of the tree of life.

In contrast to all these various forms of messianic

expectation stands a hope of an entirely different kind; the messenger of God will not come as a man—prophet, priest, or king—but will descend from heaven. This idea is first found in the book of Daniel. In the seventh chapter of that book, there is a description of the last judgment. Thrones have been set up, and the Ancient of Days (that is, God himself) has taken his seat. The judgment is held, and the books, in which everything has been recorded, are brought forth. Then follow these verses: "I saw in the night visions, and behold, with the clouds of heaven there came one like a son of man, and he came to the Ancient of Days and was presented before him. And to him was given dominion and glory and kingdom, that all peoples, nations, and languages should serve him; his dominion is an everlasting dominion, which shall not pass away, and his kingdom one that shall not be destroyed" (Daniel 7:13–14). What is set forth in these short phrases was expanded and described in greater detail in other Jewish writings, which are not included in the Old Testament as we have it: at the end of the days, the Son of man shall come down upon the clouds of heaven, take his seat upon his throne, exercise strict judgment upon the kings and mighty ones of the earth, and set his chosen people free. This expression "the Son of man" could be understood in Hebrew and Aramaic simply as referring to an ordinary man. Here, however, the title is not used in that sense; in the context of the messianic expectations of the Jews, the expression "Son of man" indicates a majesty beyond compare; the Son of man is the heavenly messenger of God, who has been with God from all eternity, and at the end of the days will be sent down from heaven to earth.

These various forms of the Jewish expectation of a Messiah were never reduced to any uniformity. All these types of messianic hope existed side by side and unconnected with one another. But in one point they all agreed—they all looked forward in the near future to a crisis in world history, to be brought about by God's direct action in the world: God will send his anointed one, and will deliver his people.

The Messianic Dignity of Jesus

Among the first Christians, these many and various forms of the Jewish messianic expectation were all applied to Jesus, and first found their unity in the church's confession of faith in him as the Christ. He is the fulfiller of all the promises, and of all the expectations directed toward the coming of the messenger of God. He is the Anointed, the Prophet, the Priest, the Son of man. Thus, Christian confession of faith in Jesus as Messiah was not determined by one definite and fixed form of the Jewish expectation; these expressions were adopted by Christians as forms in which they could express the meaning of the cross and resurrection. The various titles of dignity which were used of Jesus were intended to make clear, in one direction or another, that in Jesus Christ the Scriptures had been fulfilled.

Jesus came from Nazareth, a little town in Galilee. But who is this Jesus of Nazareth? Mark tells us at the very beginning of his book: He is the Christ (1:1). Christ, as we have said, is simply the Greek translation of the Jewish word Messiah, the anointed. Jesus is the Messiah. But in what sense is this word to be understood? Most Jews of that time expected that the Messiah, who was to be born of the family of David, would appear as a victorious king and warrior, to set the people free and to bring in the time of salvation. In Mark's Gospel, Jesus is called also the Son of David. The blind beggar before the gates of Jericho, who asks for Jesus' help, cries out to him without ceasing: "Jesus, Son of David, have mercy on me!" (10:47 ff.). He had heard that Jesus of Nazareth was passing by; therefore, he cries out at the top of his voice, in order to attract the attention of Jesus. But in what sense can this term, the Son of David, be rightly applied to Jesus? Only in one other passage of the Gospel do we meet this expression. In a dispute with the scribes, Jesus criticizes the opinion of the Jews that the Messiah is the son of David (12:35–37). "How can that be true?" he asks. In Psalm 110:1, it is written: "The Lord said to my Lord, Sit at my right hand, till I put thy enemies under thy feet." The men of that time believed that this Psalm had been written by David himself. Thus David says that the Lord (that is, God) bids Messiah (that is, my lord) take the place of honor at his right hand. This is a saying which refers to the majesty and honor which belong to Messiah. But—so Jesus argues—if David speaks of Messiah as "my lord," how can Messiah be David's son? This is impossible, since no man speaks of his own son as his lord. This is intended as a criticism of the ideas about Messiah which were held by the Jews. According to their ideas, Messiah was to appear as an earthly king; but it is never even suggested in the Gospel that Jesus had come as a Messiah of that kind. Jesus the Messiah, to whom the Gospel bears witness, is David's lord, seated at God's right hand. The risen Jesus, who has been exalted to God's right hand, is this lord; it is of Him that the words of Psalm 110 were spoken.

In spite of the criticism which Jesus had directed against the idea of Messiah as the son of David, the blind man at Jericho is recorded as having addressed Him as son of David. In what sense can this title be suitably used of Jesus? There can be no doubt that Jesus really was born in the family of David. There is clear evidence for this in many passages of the early Christian tradition (see Romans 1:3; 2 Timothy 2:8). In Romans 1:3, which is probably a quotation made by Paul from an early Christian confession of faith, it is said of Jesus that he was descended from David according to the flesh. But his dignity as Messiah is not derived from his origin; he is called the Son of David only because he did as a matter of fact belong to that family. As is clear from what follows in Romans 1:4, it is as the risen and exalted Lord that he is Messiah.

After Mark has recorded many of the miracles wrought by Jesus in the course of his ministry, he at length tells us in the eighth chapter that Jesus directly asked his disciples the question "Who do men say that I am?" "What are people saying about this Jesus?" The answers are as many and varied as were the Jewish hopes for the time of the end. Some were saying that He was John the Baptist. John had appeared as a prophet, and had then been put to death by Herod (6:17–29). But Jesus also had the appearance of a prophet, so much so that many people thought that John the Baptist had risen from the dead (6:14–16), and that in reality Jesus was no other than John. Others thought that Jesus was Elijah; for Elijah also was expected to return as the messenger of God in the last days (Malachi 4:5). Perhaps this great prophet of the Old Testament period had appeared again in Jesus. Finally, there was the third answer that Jesus was one of the prophets. He might be Jeremiah (Matthew 16:14) or one of the other prophets, whose mission it would be to call the people to repentance and to bring them back to God. Thus there was a division of opinion among the people. They all ascribe a high dignity to Jesus, but they have not understood who he is. Who then is Jesus? This question can be answered only by one who believes in him. So Jesus puts the decisive question to his disciples (8:29): "But who do *you* say that I am?" Through this question the disciples of Jesus, who have trustfully followed him, are clearly marked off from all others who remain outside. "Have *you* then understood who I am?" Peter answers on behalf of the whole group of the disciples, and says: "You are the Christ," i.e., the Messiah. This answer is remarkably brief. And what does this confession of faith in Jesus as the Messiah really mean? Without further explanation the phrase might be completely misunderstood. So Mark does not stop with this single phrase, but goes on to add another most important passage —Jesus teaches his disciples the correct understanding of the term "Messiah." For he is not a Messiah such as the Jews expected, a Messiah who, like David, would rule as king. He is rather a Messiah who must suffer, die, and rise again. In this connection the word "Messiah" is not used; instead we find another title of dignity, which in St. Mark's Gospel is found only on the lips of Jesus himself: He is the Son of man, who is entering on the way to the cross (8:31–32). He is not a political Messiah-king; his kingship is not of this world (John 18:36); he, the crucified and risen Jesus, he is the Messiah.

The term "Son of man" as a messianic title of Jesus is found not only in this passage, but also in the account of the trial of Jesus before the Sanhedrin of the Jews. In order to obtain some valid ground for the condemnation of Jesus, the high priest, who is presiding at the examination, asks him: "Are you the Christ, the Son of the Blessed?" (14:61). To this question Jesus answers: "I am; and you will see the Son of man sitting at the right hand of Power (i.e., of God), and coming with the clouds of heaven" (14:62). Jesus is the Messiah; that is to say, in terms of Mark's witness to Jesus, Jesus is the Son of man.

We have already seen that the Son of man was a figure familiar from one form of the Jewish hopes for the time of the end. The Son of man was to come in the last days to execute judgment and to set his people free. The title is found also with this meaning in some passages of Mark's Gospel. Thus, in the passage just quoted as the answer of Jesus to the question of the high priest, we read that the Son of man will come down directly from his place of honor at the right hand of God with the clouds of heaven. At the end of the days of great distress, he will come with great power and glory (13:26). In another passage, Jesus says: "Whoever is ashamed of me and of my words in this adulterous and sinful generation, of him will the Son of man also be ashamed, when he comes in the glory of his Father with the holy angels" (8:38). Thus, in the light of the attitude which a man takes now to the words of Jesus, decision has already been made as to the sentence that will be passed upon him at the last judgment.

We can see, however, from other words of Jesus which have also been recorded for us in Mark's Gospel that, like the other Jewish titles for the Messiah, the idea "Son of man" was not taken over unaltered from the Jewish tradition. The Jews thought of the Son of man only as the triumphant judge and deliverer of the people; they knew nothing of the truth that he must suffer and be killed. In general, he is expected only as the victorious hero and warrior. But the idea of a Messiah who is hanged on a cross had not entered into anyone's imagination.

Jesus is the Son of man who suffers, dies, and rises again. For this reason the title "Son of man" acquires a new weight, a new significance beyond compare. To Peter's confession "Thou art the Christ," Jesus replies by telling the disciples what is involved in this confession of faith in him as Messiah. For "the Son of man must suffer many things, and be rejected by the elders and the chief priests and the scribes, and be killed, and after three days rise again" (8:31; cf. 9:31; 10:33–34). Three times these words are repeated at short intervals. Like deep notes of a bell, these phrases echo throughout the whole of the rest of the Gospel—we are going up to Jerusalem, and the Son of man must be crucified. Three times this affirmation is repeated, and thereby set forth in its unalterable validity. The reader may find himself reminded of the way in which the voice of God called Samuel three times, until he was willing to answer "Speak, Lord, for thy servant hears" (1 Samuel 3:1–10). Jesus is the obedient Servant, who knows and fulfills God's will. He walks in that way of which the prophet had written: "Surely he has borne our griefs and carried our sorrows; yet we esteemed him stricken, smitten by God, and afflicted. But he was wounded for our transgressions, he was bruised for our iniquities; upon him was the chastisement that made us whole, and with his stripes we are healed. Therefore I will divide him a portion with the great, and he shall divide the spoil with the strong; because he poured out his soul to death, and was numbered with the transgressors; yet he bore the sin of many, and made intercession for the transgressors" (Isaiah 53:4, 5, 12). A strange kind of Messiah, whose glory is to be found precisely in his sufferings, and whose majesty is seen in his obedience. According to God's will it must be so, that the Son of man suffers and is rejected (9:12), that he goes his way (14:21) and that he is delivered up into the hands of sinners (14:41). But why must it be so?

The answer to this question is given in the saying of Jesus: "The Son of man also came not to be served but to serve, and to give his life as a ransom for many" (10:45). Here are stated the commission of Jesus and the purpose of his ministry. He serves as the obedient Servant, as that servant had been foretold and depicted in Isaiah 53. He gave his life "for many." That means "for all." There is, in fact, in the Semitic languages (Hebrew, Aramaic, etc.) no word which exactly expresses the idea "all men." A writer in those languages who wished to speak of something that concerns all men could express his meaning only by using the term "the many." So it is in this utterance of Jesus. The words "the many" do not mean that one group or another among mankind is excluded; on the contrary, all are included; the Son of man has endured the cross for all men. He is not only the Messiah of Israel, the ancient people of God; he is the Savior of all the world. That is his commission. In obedience to the will of God, he offers up his life as a ransom. The word "ransom" recalls a regulation of the old law—that a life which was forfeit could be bought back by the payment of a ransom (Exodus 21:30; Numbers 35:31). But it is impossible for men to pay off by means of a ransom the guilt in which they have become involved in relation to God (Psalm 49:8). Each man must die himself the death that he has deserved. What can a man give in exchange for his life? (8:37). He can never pay the price. But this saying of Jesus affirms that the Son of man has come to serve, and to give his life as a ransom for the deliverance of all men. That which none of them can do, he does on their behalf; he pays the ransom in their stead. He takes upon himself the death which they have all deserved through their guilt in the sight of God. He dies in their stead, in order that they all may be free.

Jesus is the crucified Messiah, whom God has raised from the dead. As the obedient Servant he is raised to the position of honor at the right hand of God (12:10 ff.). Therefore glory and majesty beyond compare are ascribed to him as Son of man. Through the authority given to him by God he does that which, according to Jewish ideas, not even the Messiah could do: "But that you may know that the Son of man has authority on earth to forgive sins—he said to the paralytic: 'I say to you, rise, take up your pallet and go home'" (2:10–11). According to the Jewish expectation, the Messiah is to be subject to the law, and to observe it in every point and in every detail with careful exactness; the authority of Jesus, however, is greater than that of the law: "the Son of man is lord even of the sabbath" (2:28). Thus the title "Son of man" sets forth plainly the messianic dignity of Jesus, and the authority which he had received from God.

We find in St. Mark's Gospel another title of honor used of Jesus; and this is in fact the highest point reached by the Evangelist in the confession of faith in Jesus Christ: He is the Son of God. At his first appearance Jesus is addressed by this title. After he has been baptized by John the Baptist, a voice from heaven is heard saying: "Thou art my beloved Son; with thee I am well pleased" (1:11). Here two passages of the Old Testament are brought together and applied to Jesus—Psalm 2:7 and Isaiah 42:1. He is the One in whom the Scriptures are fulfilled. His messianic dignity is openly declared at the outset of his ministry. The baptism is not to be viewed as a self-dedication of Jesus to the office of Messiah; here, at the beginning of his book, Mark makes it clear to us that "God was in Christ reconciling the world to himself" (2 Corinthians 5:19). The Son of God comes to the community of sinners; the Servant takes their burden upon himself and bears it in their stead. Just as at the beginning of his ministry Jesus is greeted as Son of God, so also at the end. Beneath the cross on which Jesus has died is standing a heathen centurion who has seen all that has happened. He is the first to confess faith in the Crucified, and cries out: "Truly this man was a son of God" (15:39).

Before men begin to confess Jesus by this name, the

evil spirits, on whom he has declared war, have done so. They have, as it appears, more than earthly knowledge, and know who he is (3:11; 5:7). In ancient times, it was generally believed that the knowledge of a name gave the one who knew it power over the one who bore that name. A certain magical power goes with the utterance of the name. So, when the evil spirits cry out: "We know who you are, the Son of God," this does not mean that they are greeting Jesus with joy. On the contrary, the use of the Name seems to be intended as a charm, through which they hope to prevent the power of Jesus from being exercised against themselves. But no exorcism or calling upon the Name is of any avail to the evil spirits. When the Son of God appears, their power is at an end. He triumphs over principalities and powers, and brings their dominion to an end.

In the scene on the mount of transfiguration, where the future glory of Jesus is made known in advance to the disciples, the same voice is heard as was heard at the baptism: "This is my beloved Son: listen to him" (9:7). Jesus is the Christ, the Messiah, the Son of God (14:61 ff.). In a parable (12:1–12) the nature of the mission of the Son is set forth. A certain man had a vineyard, which he let out to tenants. He himself left the district. But when the time had come that he should receive from the tenants his share of the produce, he several times sent servants to them. But the tenants beat and killed the messengers of their lord. That is exactly what the people of Israel had done to the prophets, whom God had sent to them. Now the lord of the vineyard had one beloved son. Finally, he sent him to demand of the vinedressers the portion which belonged to the lord. But the tenants did not reverence even the son; they said "This is the heir; come, let us kill him." So they took him, and killed him, and cast him out of the vineyard. This is what Israel did with the Son, whom in the end God sent to them, after he had spoken to them in vain by so many prophets. They nailed the Son to the cross.

Jesus is the Son of God. He is not merely endued with divine power; he is like God in his nature. He addresses God as his Father, because he is his Son (14:36). This is the highest expression which can be used to make plain his messianic dignity. But God's Son humbles himself, and as the obedient Servant endures the cross. He reveals his glory as it were beneath a veil, so that only the eyes of those who believe are able to recognize him. It is only the man who, beneath this veil, can recognize the glory of the Messiah who belongs to the fellowship of Jesus.

Jesus is aware that he has been sent to the whole people of Israel. He gathers twelve disciples about him (3:13–19). This number is not capriciously chosen. It corresponds to the twelve tribes of the ancient people of God. The good news is to be proclaimed to the whole people. He sends out his messengers, in order that they may rapidly proclaim the good tidings everywhere (6:7–13). But the fate of the disciples will be in no way different from the fate of their Master. The man who follows him must also be prepared to take up his cross (8:34). This phrase has nothing to do with putting up with a number of inconveniences; it points to martyrdom, to bearing the cross as Jesus had borne it. In the time of Jesus the man who was condemned to death had himself to carry the wood of his cross to the place of execution. Of those who follow him, Jesus demands this ultimate willingness to surrender themselves and to follow him alone. They are asked whether they are willing to drink from the same cup as he, and to be baptized with the baptism with which he has been baptized (10:38). That means the willingness to die. For suffering can come upon a man as a flood and can completely overwhelm him (see Psalm 42:7; 69:2). It is evident that Jesus is here speaking of the baptism of death, which he himself has to undergo. In obedience he has drunk of the cup (14:36), and as Son has fulfilled the will of the Father.

chapter **4**

The Acts of Jesus

Jesus as the Helper of the Sick

THE earliest Christian preaching concerning Jesus as the Christ did not deal only with the cross and resurrection; as we have seen, it included also the mighty works which he had wrought: "He went about doing good and healing all that were oppressed by the devil, for God was with him" (Acts 10:38). Of these acts of Jesus, Mark gives us a considerable number of graphic examples. "He healed all that were possessed of the devil." The evil spirits were the first to address Jesus as Son of God, because they wished to obtain power over him by this form of address. But Jesus was stronger than they. He drove out the devils and delivered them over to destruction (5:1–20). These acts of Jesus created a sensation, and exposed him to the reproach that he was driving out the devils with the help of the prince of the devils, that he had made a covenant with Beelzebul (3:22). What was meant by this reproach was that Jesus could perform such miracles only with the help of the power of Satan. Jesus rejected this accusation with all possible vigor. How could

Satan drive out Satan? For, if he was overcoming the devils with the help of the devils, that was what was happening. If his enemies were right, that would mean that the kingdom of Satan had become divided against itself, and so was doomed to destruction. Now it was the fact that the kingdom of Satan was nearing its end, for One who was stronger than he had broken into his house, and had bound the strong man (3:22–27). The victories of Jesus over the demons, through which he robbed them of their power, are thus a sign that the dominion of Satan has been broken, and that Jesus has won the victory over him.

"He did good." This was what was said of Jesus in the early Christian preaching. He went here and there through the countryside, and healed the sick, the lame, the blind, the deaf and dumb. A story is told of a deaf and dumb man being brought to Jesus (7:31–37). The people who bring the sick man are at the end of their resources; they know of nothing more that they can do to help him. Therefore, they ask Jesus to lay his hands on the head of the man who is deaf and dumb—perhaps that will help. Jesus does as they ask him. He leads the man to one side and separates him from the crowd. The sentences which follow describe exactly the technique used by Jesus in performing the miracle. He puts his fingers into the deaf ears, as though by this means he wished to open up the channels of hearing. He spits and touches the speechless tongue, as though it was his purpose thereby to loose the bands which had so far hindered the utterance of speech. We find very similar descriptions in accounts of healings from non-Christian sources. But what gives its character to the act of Jesus is not a particular technique of healing. Next Jesus looks up to heaven, sighs, and speaks with divine authority the word of deliverance: "Ephphatha, be opened." This command is not addressed only to the sick organs of hearing and speech; it is a call to the whole man to be opened, and to recognize that it is the Lord who stands before him. "And his ears were opened, his tongue was released, and he spoke plainly." Thus it is recorded of the obedience that follows upon the command of Christ.

What is the significance of this, and other stories of healing which Mark records? We find stories of miracles in the records of many religions; they are by no means to be found only in the ministry of Jesus. The Evangelist himself knows well that false prophets also can perform signs and wonders (13:22). If we wish to understand the meaning of these miracles of Jesus, we must not overlook what comes at the end of this story: "And they were astonished beyond measure, saying, 'He has done all things well; he even makes the deaf hear and the dumb speak'" (7:37). At the end of the story comes an outburst of praise from all those who had seen the mighty work of Jesus. But what is the content of this outburst of praise? It takes up words which are to be found in the Old Testament. In the book of Isaiah, the prophet foretells the time of salvation that is to come: "Then the eyes of the blind shall be opened, and the ears of the deaf unstopped; then shall the lame man leap like a hart, and the tongue of the dumb sing for joy. For waters shall break forth in the wilderness, and streams in the desert" (Isaiah 35:5–6). These words are now fulfilled—that is the content of the song of praise that is raised by the fellowship of those who have believed in Jesus. He is the One in whom the promises of the Old Testament have become present reality, in whom the world of God's salvation comes near. Thus the miracles of Jesus are signs that make it plain that he is the Messiah.

In this story there is another sentence which we have not yet considered. Immediately after the healing, according to the account given by St. Mark, Jesus charged the people to tell no one of what they had seen (7:36). A similar command is found in other passages of St. Mark. For instance, when Jesus has healed a leper, he bids him: "See that you say nothing to any one" (1:44). When the evil spirits address him as Son of God, he orders them strictly not to make him known (3:12). After he has raised the daughter of Jairus, he strictly charges those present that no one should know this (5:43). This idea—that the mighty works of Jesus were not done in order that they might be generally known but that they were intended to be kept secret—runs right through Mark's Gospel. No doubt Jesus is revealing his dignity as Messiah, but it is as though a veil of secrecy had to be spread over the revelation of his majesty. When, on the mount of transfiguration, his future glory shines through, Jesus bids his disciples tell no man what they have seen, until the Son of man should have risen from the dead (9:9).

In this word we can find the key to the understanding of the special idea, set forth in the Gospel of Mark, of "the secret of the Messiah." Only those who have believed in Jesus as the crucified and risen Christ can understand the truth that Jesus of Nazareth is the Messiah. Apart from this faith, there can be no true confession of him as Messiah. The earthly activity of Jesus is covered by a thin veil of secrecy; the purpose of all this is simply to make clear that, apart from Good Friday and Easter, there can be no confession of faith in Jesus Christ. For this reason, his miracles cannot be understood in separation from his death and resurrection. The cross and the resurrection alone throw light upon them, and make it possible for us to understand their meaning and their purpose.

If these sayings, in which Jesus commanded silence, had really had no other purpose than to keep something secret, it is evident that they entirely failed of their purpose. In the story, to which we have referred in detail, they have in fact just the contrary effect: "The more he charged them, the more zealously they proclaimed it" (7:36). Then follows the outburst of praise on which we have already commented. And when Jesus the conqueror of death has restored the little daughter of Jairus to life, in spite of the command to keep silence no one can have remained unaware that the child who had died had been brought back to life again (5:43). These words of Jesus, then, which Mark records in several contexts, are intended to remind us that he who wrought these miracles was the same Jesus whose cross and resurrection were the subject of the early Christian preaching. It is he who is the conqueror of death, suffering, and sin.

The common opinion of the Jews in the time of Jesus was that there was a close connection between sickness and sin. It was supposed that it was possible to infer that a sick man must also be a great sinner, since such suffering could come upon him only as a punishment for guilt in the sight of God. Jesus absolutely rejected this Jewish way of calculating and balancing sickness against sin. Certainly there is a connection between sickness and sin, since we may think that if there had been no sin, there would be no sickness in the world, though this connection between guilt and suffering is something of which, in the individual case, we men are not able to judge. For this reason, Jesus said to the paralyzed man who was brought to him: "Your sins are forgiven" (2:5). With the forgiveness of sins, the root of the sickness also has been cut. But, in order to make it clear that he has authority to forgive men their sins, he adds: "Rise, take up your pallet and go home." "And he rose, and immediately took up the pallet and went out before them all; so that they were all amazed and glorified God, saying, 'We never saw anything like this!' " (2:12).

The healings of sick persons and of those possessed by evil spirits are not the only miracles of Jesus that are recorded in this Gospel; we find also records of miracles in which his power over nature is revealed.

The disciples are crossing the lake of Gennesaret with Jesus. A violent storm breaks out; the waves rise higher and higher, and end by beating into the boat. Jesus is sitting at the stern of the boat and is asleep. In their distress, the disciples wake the Master, and ask him why he shows no concern about the fact that they are in danger of drowning. Jesus awakes, rebukes the wind, and says to the sea, "Peace! Be still!" Then the wind ceases, and there is a great calm. Jesus rebukes the disciples for their despair and for their lack of faith. How could they be so anxious and troubled, when after all the Lord was with them all the time in the boat? Then they were filled with awe, and said one to another: "Who then is this, that even wind and sea obey him?" (4:35–41). Who then is he? Through their lack of faith the disciples were not able to grasp it. To faith alone the secret is revealed. He is the Lord. And he is with his own. Therefore, in all the storms which break upon them, they can be calm and confident. If the Lord is with them in the boat, then those who believe in him need have no fear. Wind and sea alike must obey him.

Mark twice tells us how Jesus supplied food to a great crowd of people which had gathered about him (6:34–44; 8:1–9). The two accounts are alike in all the main points, though the number of those who were fed is given differently in the two accounts. But in both cases the circumstances are exactly the same. Jesus is in a lonely place, and it is already late in the day. A great crowd has gathered to hear the preaching of Jesus. The disciples have no idea how they can be fed. They think that the best plan is to send the people away and let them look after themselves. But how can they do so, in such a lonely place? Jesus gives the command that they are to be fed. But how is this to be managed? There are only five loaves and two small fishes. Bread and fish were commonly eaten at the simple meals which the poor folk prepared for themselves. The loaves were about as large as a plate, and as thick as a man's thumb—no larger. Jesus arranges for the people to sit down in orderly groups on the green grass. Then Jesus did exactly what the head of a Jewish family regularly did—taking the bread, praying over it, thanking God for the gift of the food, and then breaking the bread and distributing it. He divides the bread and gives it to the disciples. They in turn distribute it to the people until all are satisfied. Only at the end of the story is the greatness of the miracle made plain; twelve baskets full of the broken fragments are gathered up—far more than there had been at the beginning of the meal. Who then is this Jesus, who can feed a great multitude of men?

We find elsewhere stories of the feeding of crowds, and they occur also in the Old Testament (1 Kings 17:8–16; 2 Kings 4:1–7, 42–44). What is the special significance of this miracle of Jesus? It is a revelation of the mercy of God, since Jesus comes as the shepherd of the flock (6:34), the good shepherd who cares for the sheep (Psalm 23:1). Many may fail to understand this. Those who observe only the outward appearance will see only the peaceful picture of the resting crowd, taking their meal sitting on the green grass. But the disciples recognize who this Jesus is who has provided the meal. At the end, they see the greatness of the miracle in which he has revealed his glory. To faith is revealed the understanding of this story, which clearly points forward to that last meal which Jesus was to take in company with his disciples. And, beyond that meal, it looks still further forward to the holy Supper which the church observes, and in which Jesus the Lord is present as he who breaks and distributes the bread (see also Luke 24:13–35). "He looked up to heaven, and blessed, and broke the loaves, and gave them to the disciples" (6:41).

Mark tells us that in the last days in Jerusalem, Jesus through a final miracle revealed once more to the disciples who he is. They passed by a fig tree, on which there were leaves only but no fruit. This was not surprising, since it was not the season of the year at which fruit was to be expected. And yet Jesus cursed the fig tree, and said "May no one ever eat fruit from you again" (11:11–14). Next morning, when Jesus and his disciples again passed by the fig tree, it was completely withered (11:20 ff.). A strange story! It can be understood only if the symbolic meaning, which lies within it, is recognized. Israel is the fig tree, on which fruit is sought in vain (see Hosea 9:10, 16; Micah 7:1). In no other case is a miracle of Jesus recorded that was not of help and service to other men. This is the only example of a cursing miracle. Therefore, this story can be understood only in terms of the inner meaning which is represented by the outward act. When so understood, in its setting immediately before the passion of Jesus, it is seen to carry an extremely serious message. Judgment is coming upon Israel, because it bears no fruit, because it has failed to recognize and to accept the Christ of God, because it has rejected him and condemned him to the cross. Judgment has already been passed upon the unbelieving people of God. For Jesus is the Lord, and he who rejects Him has fallen away from the living God, and is destined to wither away.

The Controversies of Jesus with His Enemies

The effect of the mighty works of Jesus, his miracles and his healing of the sick, was to arouse against him many adversaries, who bitterly attacked him. They accuse him of having performed his mighty works with the help of Satan (3:22), and demand of him a sign to establish beyond the possibility of doubt his claim to be the Messiah. Jesus rejects this demand. His miracles are not a proof, intended to compel men to believe; they are not a problem in mathematics, which can be calculated and worked out. The miracles of Jesus are signs of his messianic dignity and a challenge to faith. Therefore, it is only through faith that it is possible to understand what takes place in the mighty works of Jesus.

Who are these enemies of Jesus, who are offended by his actions and by the message that he proclaims? They are not godless and unbelieving folk; on the contrary, they are the very people who wish to be pious and God-fearing, or at least to give the impression of being such. They simply could not understand how it could come about that Jesus could forgive sins, how it could come about that he could eat with sinners and enter into fellowship with them (2:1–12, 15–28). Along with sinners, the publicans are frequently mentioned. At that time no one had a worse reputation than the publicans. They were in the service of the heathen power of Rome, the ruling power in the land. Besides, they were deceitful men, who extracted as much money as possible from the people who had to pass by the stations where they collected custom and tolls. No man of good position wished to have anything to do with these publicans. But Jesus, who has come on behalf of all men, comes also to the publicans, and gives to them the privilege of entering into fellowship with himself. The respectable people simply could not understand this. How was it possible that the Messiah should do anything of the kind, that he should spend his time with outcasts, with men of ill repute? They would not admit that Jesus could bring to such people also the joy of God.

As a result, Jesus finds himself engaged in sharp controversies with those who are opposed to him. Who are these opponents? In Mark we meet first the scribes (2:6; see also 2:16; 3:22; 7:5; 11:27; 12:28–34, etc.). These were the professional theologians of that time. They had spent their lives in the study of the Scriptures, and made it their aim to deduce from the Scriptures the will of God for their own times. They were diligent in study; they believed themselves to have grasped the rules in accordance with which alone God would act. But they had become vain, and had turned to seek the honor that comes from men. They thought it possible, on the basis of their knowledge, to set limits to the will of God (12:38–40).

The actions of Jesus do not fit in with their understanding of the Scriptures. From the law, the scribes had worked out a very large number of commands and prohibitions—613 in all—all of which, without exception, the pious Jew was expected to observe. A considerable number of these rules were concerned simply with the keeping of the Sabbath day (2:23—3:6). It is not surprising, therefore, that a scribe puts to Jesus the question as to which is the most important of these many commandments (12:28). Jesus replies with two passages from Scripture: "Thou shalt love the Lord thy God" (Deuteronomy 6:5) and "Thou shalt love thy neighbour as thyself" (Leviticus 19:18). There is no other command which can be compared with this single command to love. But the scribes did not practice the love of their neighbors. They declared bitter war on Jesus because he received the sinners and the sick, and decided to destroy him as soon as they had the opportunity (3:22; 11:18; 14:1).

With the scribes, the Pharisees were also among the bitter enemies of Jesus (2:16, 18, 24; 3:6; 7:1–5; 8:11; 10:2; 12:13–17, etc.). Their name "Pharisees" meant "those who were set apart." They had separated themselves from the mass of the people, and had gathered themselves together in a fellowship of the pious. They wished to represent the community of the truly pious Jews, who fulfilled the law of God down to the last detail with careful exactness. They really worked hard to put their convictions into practice. They fasted twice in the week, though no command could be quoted from the Old Testament requiring them to do so (2:18). They gave away conscientiously the tenth part of all that they earned or received (see Luke 18:12). They observed not only the laws, as they were set forth in the Old Testament, but also "the tradition of the elders" (7:3). That is to say, they accepted as valid the rules of the Old Testament, as they had been explained, expanded, and multiplied by the scribes. It was not laid down anywhere in the Old Testament that the ordinary Jew must undergo a ritual washing on every kind of occasion. But the Pharisees carried out the rules which had originally been laid down only for the priests, since they wished to be the fellowship of the pure, who kept themselves holy unto the Lord (7:3–5). They formed themselves into groups, in order as far as possible to have to do only with those who shared their convictions, and to have nothing to do with ordinary folk whom they regarded as sinners. These groups were generally under the direction of one or more of the scribes. Thus in 2:16 we read of "scribes of the Pharisees." The Pharisees themselves were lay folk, many of them being peasants or artisans.

These people tried, in their own fashion, to do the will of God. But Jesus saw through to their hearts. They were proud and arrogant. And underneath their pious manner of living was hypocrisy. They were not really seeking God but themselves. With their lips they honored God, but their heart was far from him (7:6–13).

Along with the scribes and Pharisees, we find the Sadducees also as enemies of Jesus. They belonged to the upper classes of society, and had their followers among the rich. The high priest and the chief priests of the temple at Jerusalem were Sadducees. In contrast to the Pharisees, they did not accept the tradition of the elders; they held conservatively to the letter of the Old Testament. The Sadducees did not believe in the resurrection of the dead, because there was no clear evidence for it in the Old Testament. This was the subject of a dispute between Jesus and the Sadducees. Jesus meets their chilly skepticism with a sharp attack, based on a quotation from the Scriptures. In Exodus 3:6 it is written: "I am the God of Abraham, the God of Isaac, and the God of Jacob." If God in this word spoken to Moses links his own name with the names of Abraham, Isaac, and Jacob, then these three men cannot be forever dead, since God is the God of the living and not of the dead (12:18–27). Jesus is here arguing in line with the methods followed by the scribes, and expounds the Scriptures in accordance with the rules that were regarded as valid at that time. But the meaning of his utterance is quite clear; the fact that God is God is the guarantee for the resurrection of the dead. With this argument, Jesus wards off the attack of the Sadducees.

All who at that time held high rank and position were joined together against Jesus. Among them were the elders, the heads of the leading families in Jerusalem. Together with the chief priests and scribes they made up the membership of the Sanhedrin, which, under the high priest as president, was the chief governing authority of the Jewish people. The pious and the rich will have nothing to do with the Nazarene. He threatens to destroy the world which they have built up for themselves. They are his bitter enemies, because Jesus has exposed their hypocrisy and called them to repentance. They are not willing to obey this call, and prefer to silence the One who utters it. Although there were many and deep differences of opinion among them, they were all at one in their enmity against Jesus. And yet it was through this enmity, and through the impulses of men, that God was bringing his plan to accomplishment. For "the Son of man must suffer many things, and be rejected by the elders and the chief priests and the scribes, and be killed, and after three days rise again" (8:31).

chapter 5

The Message That Jesus Proclaimed

The Authority of Jesus

JESUS moved about the country from place to place, as was the custom of the scribes. He gathered about himself a band of pupils; he studied the Scriptures of the Old Testament and expounded them. In this respect he gave the impression of being one of the scribes. He was called "teacher" as they were (4:38); the title of honor "Rabbi" was addressed to him as it was to them (John 3:2, etc.). But what he says and does is quite different from what the scribes said and did. His teaching is with authority, and not like that of the scribes. He is not dependent on the opinions of men; he directly declares God's will, so that all who hear him are astonished (1:21 ff.).

The first saying with which, in Mark's account, Jesus begins his preaching sums up the whole of his message in a single sentence: "The time is fulfilled, and the kingdom of God is at hand; repent, and believe in the gospel" (1:15). The time is fulfilled—just as a vessel is full when it has been filled up to the very brim. Jesus comes in the fullness of the time (Galatians 4:4). That can only mean that Jesus is *the* revelation of God; after him there can be no other. For in him the measure of the time is fulfilled. The kingdom of God has drawn near. Every Jew would be able to understand at once what that meant: "Your God reigns." That was the heart of the good news which the messenger of joy was to bring to the people of Zion (Isaiah 52:7).

God as Creator had established his kingly rule over heaven and earth. But, as Israel well knew, his kingly rule upon earth has been broken. Men have for the most part refused to obey him. Unbelief and satanic powers have spread themselves abroad through the earth. Only the fellowship of believers knows that God is king and that in reality he continues to rule. Therefore, that fellowship waits with eager longing for the day when God will establish his kingdom visibly throughout the earth; then the message of joy will ring out: "God has brought in his kingdom." This royal rule of God will mean the end of suffering, and of all sin, sickness, and guilt. The expression "the kingdom of God" in this connection does not mean an empire with definite boundaries, one particular country. God's kingdom is anywhere where God is king—and to that no boundaries can be prescribed. And he makes his kingdom visible on earth when and as he wills. Jesus says "the kingdom of God is at hand." By so saying, he identifies himself as the expected messenger of the good news. God's kingdom comes through Jesus Christ, and is present wherever his word is believed. To this proclamation is added the command "Repent." This word does not demand simply a change of mind or of point of view; the word which in the Old Testament is used for repentance might more accurately be translated "conversion" (see Amos 4:6–13; Jeremiah 26:3; 36:3, 7, etc.). Turn right about! So far you have been going in exactly the wrong direction. Make a complete change in your ways. How is this possible? Conversion is possible, because in Jesus Christ, God has drawn near to men. Therefore, believe in the good news; put your trust in it; accept it!

If we look at the Gospel of Mark as a whole, we shall see that much more space is given in it to stories about the mighty works of Jesus than to examples of his preaching. What Jesus said and taught is set forth for us in much fuller form in the Gospels of Matthew and Luke. Mark gives his preference to the mighty works, because it was in these that Jesus revealed his glory; in these it is evident that he is the crucified and risen Lord. But in many of the miracle-stories which he records, the interest of the Evangelist is not so much in the event as such, as in the word of Jesus by which it is accompanied. It is the word of Jesus that is victorious over the demons, over sickness, and over sin. The crucial point of the stories which tell of the mighty works of Jesus is always to be found in the word: "Ephphatha—Be opened" (7:34); "Do not fear, only believe" (5:36). In such words, to which many other examples could be added from the miracle-stories, is revealed the significance of the mighty work of Jesus. They are a call to faith, an invitation to accept the good news.

The words of Jesus and his acts are thus closely related to one another. Jesus teaches with authority. His word is so mighty that it pierces home, and causes amazement in those who hear it. In the controversies which Jesus has with his opponents, his word is always victorious, and robs his opponents of their weapons. At the end of each of the disputes recorded in Chapters 2 and 3 is found a saying of Jesus. If we place these sayings together, they make plain to us the authority of Jesus and the nature of his claims: "My son, your sins are forgiven"

(2:5). "That you may know that the Son of man has authority on earth to forgive sins—he said to the paralytic —'I say to you, rise, take up your pallet and go home' " (2:10 ff.). "Those who are well have no need of a physician, but those who are sick; I came not to call the righteous, but sinners" (2:17). "Can the wedding guests fast while the bridegroom is with them? As long as they have the bridegroom with them, they cannot fast" (2:17, 19). "The sabbath was made for man, not man for the sabbath; so the Son of man is lord even of the sabbath" (2:27 f.). "Is it lawful on the sabbath to do good or to do harm, to save life or to kill?" (3:4). These words make evident the claim and the authority of Jesus. Some accept his teaching and believe in him; others decide to crucify him (3:6). It is clear that there can be no neutrality where he is concerned.

He teaches with authority. The controversies of the last days in Jerusalem give a clear picture of this. When asked by the Pharisees whether it is right to pay tribute to the emperor in Rome, he has a Roman coin brought to him, and asks: "Whose likeness and inscription is this?" (12:16). To this the Pharisees themselves have to answer "The emperor's." If they have had the idea of catching Jesus in a trap through their question, they find themselves quickly put to rout: "Render to Caesar the things that are Caesar's, and to God the things that are God's" (12:17). In just the same way he routs the Sadducees, who had tried to show by an artificial question that belief in the resurrection of the dead is unreasonable. Jesus maintains against them that God is not the God of the dead but of the living (12:27). To the question as to which is the greatest commandment in the law, Jesus points to love of God and love of one's neighbor as the fulfillment of the will of God (12:29–31).

In these controversies, the authority of Jesus is seen

in the way in which he always wins these battles of words with his enemies. But the words which he speaks to his disciples are of a quite different kind. They are instructions; they are made up of directions to guide the faith and conduct of Christians. He warns them that the Son of man must suffer and die and rise again (8:31, 9:31). He calls them to follow him (8:34). He urges the disciples not to let their hearts be drawn away by the riches of this world, but to enter poor into the kingdom of God (10:17–31). He tells them that the highest among them is the servant of all; for the Son of man also came not to be served but to serve, and to give his life as a ransom for many (10:42–45).

The Kingdom of God

The kingdom of God is at hand! What is this kingdom of God, which Jesus proclaims, and which has drawn near to men in him? Mark gives us information about its nature by recording for us three parables of Jesus.

A sower went out to sow. Some seed fell by the wayside, and the birds came and carried it away. Other seed fell on rocky ground, where there was not enough earth for it to take root; under the burning heat of the sun, the seed withered. Yet other seed fell among thorns, and the thorns grew up and choked it. Finally, some seed fell in good ground, and bore fruit—thirtyfold and sixtyfold and a hundredfold (4:3–9).

If we are to understand the parable, it is important to realize that in Palestine the seed was sown before the ground had been ploughed up. So it may easily happen that some seed falls on the path, and then is not turned under by the plough; or it may happen that there is a thin layer of earth over rocks, so that the sower sows the seed there without realizing what he is doing. Only after the seed has been sown is the ground turned over by the plough. But even when we have taken account of this method of sowing, it seems very strange indeed that three-quarters of the seed sown should be wasted. Failure seems to be the normal result of this method of sowing. And, in fact, failure is what normally follows upon the preaching of the Word of God. But in spite of all ill success, the harvest comes, the sowing is not in vain. Special emphasis is laid upon the words with which the parable ends—thirtyfold, sixtyfold, a hundredfold. By contrast, this yield is very much more than the normal. So there is a sharp contrast between the partial failure and the rich harvest that is reaped. What is the meaning of this parable? God's Word is the seed, which in spite of all ill success does in the end bring forth fruit. His Word is never spoken in vain; the kingdom of God advances, in spite of all the resistance that men oppose to it.

So far we have considered the parable without reference to the interpretation of it given in verses 13–20. Here the parable is explained clause by clause, that is, allegorically. But this was not the method usually followed by Jesus in his teaching in parables; generally there is one point of comparison, by which the whole meaning of the parable is determined. This will become clearer when we consider the other parables in Mark 4. Here the various parts of the parable are interpreted as referring to different classes of men. In some, Satan steals away the Word as soon as it has been sown. Others receive the Word with joy, but they are men of a moment, and never take deep root. In the first persecution that threatens, they are offended and fall away. A third group has heard the Word, but when cares and enticements come, then the Word is choked and becomes unfruitful. Those who are sown on the good ground are those who hear the Word, receive it, and bring forth fruit. What are we to think of this interpretation of the parable? We can see that it corresponds closely to the experiences of the Christian fellowship: the Word is received (e.g., 1 Thessalonians 1:6, etc.), often with joy; but then follows persecution; Satan hinders the progress of the Word (1 Thessalonians 2:18; 3:5); the preaching of the Word results in offense (1 Peter 2:8); nevertheless, in spite of all, the Word makes progress (Acts 6:7). We might collect a whole series of passages from the New Testament showing how closely 4:13–20 corresponds to the experiences of the young Christian groups. It is probable that at a very early date this detailed interpretation of the parable was worked out, in order to make a link between the words of Jesus and the situation in which the hearers of the preaching found themselves. In the main point, the parable and the interpretation are at one—that, in spite of all failure, the Word of God goes forward to the fulfillment of his purpose, and brings forth fruit.

The two other parables are recorded without interpretation, but instead are provided with an introductory phrase to make clear to the reader the sense in which they are to be read: "The kingdom of God is as if . . ."; then follows a parable that makes plain something in the nature of the kingdom: "as if a man should scatter seed upon the ground, and should sleep and rise night and day, and the seed should sprout and grow, he knows not how. The earth produces of itself, first the blade, then the ear, then the full grain in the ear. But when the grain is ripe, at once he puts in the sickle, because the harvest has come" (4:26–29). The earth brings forth fruit of itself ("automatically" is the word in Greek). It is on this that the emphasis is laid. This parable is closely connected with that of the sower. It is as certain that God's kingdom will come as that sowing will be followed by harvest. The parable ends with words from the Old Testament, which must be read in their context (Joel 3:13). The harvest is judgment, the judgment of God. The turning point of the ages, which is brought in through the kingship of God and his judgment, comes with the harvest.

Once more a parable is given to make clear the nature of the kingdom of God. It is like a mustard seed, which when sown is the smallest of all seeds. Yet when it is sown it grows up and becomes the greatest of all shrubs, and puts forth large branches, so that the birds of the air can make nests in its shade (4:32). Here, as in the preceding parable, a sharp contrast is set forth between the tiny seed and the large bush. Nothing is said about a slow process of growth, in which the development from one to the other takes place. There is just the contrast between the little seed and the tree under which the birds of the air find rest (see Ezekiel 17:22 ff.; 31:6; Daniel 4:9–18). The kingdom of God is here compared with this great tree. The contrast throws into relief the greatness of the wonder of the kingdom of God, which embraces all the world and all nations in its scope.

Who can understand the meaning of these parables? In themselves, they seem to present pictures which are simple and easy to understand. Yet only one who believes in Jesus as the Christ can understand what it is all about. This is the subject of verses 10–12, in which a contrast is made between the disciples and those who are outside: "To you has been given the secret of the kingdom of God, but for those outside everything is in parables." A secret has been revealed to the disciples; God himself has made it plain to them. But what *is* this secret? It is the secret of the kingdom of God. If we consider all that we have learned about the kingdom of God in the Gospel of Mark, this can only mean that the disciples have understood that, in and with the coming of Jesus Christ, the kingdom of God has already come. They understand this, because God has opened their eyes to recognize that the Crucified is also the Christ. One whose eyes have not been opened cannot understand this, even though he sees it with his eyes. This is the fulfillment of the word of the prophet of old time: "that they may indeed see but not perceive, and may indeed hear but not understand; lest they should turn again, and be forgiven" (Isaiah 6:9–10). This is a hard saying. But it was not spoken in order to arouse in men's minds anxious questionings as to whether they belonged to the company of the elect or not. The saying is directed to the disciples of Jesus, to those who believe in him, in order to warn them of their responsibility. He that has ears to hear, let him hear! If the secret of the kingdom of God has been revealed to a man, let him not at any price give up that treasure. To you has been given the secret of the kingdom of God—the dark background of the utterance of the prophet Isaiah gives a deeper emphasis to the words.

Mark introduces the parables after a series of conflict-stories, in which Jesus is seen engaged in sharp controversy with his enemies. There is a real significance in the order in which these sections are arranged. The failure, which seems to be marked by the stories of conflict and by the decision of the enemies of Jesus to destroy him, is not the end. The cross is not the end. Just as the seed, in spite of all ill success, does in the end bring forth fruit, just as the mustard seed does grow into the great bush, so after three days the Crucified will be raised up, and will triumph over death.

The Coming Lord

In early Christian preaching the expectation of the return of Jesus played a great part. The crucified and risen Lord will come again as judge of the living and the dead. The church also looked forward eagerly to the day when it would once again be united with its Lord (1 Thessalonians 1:9–10; 4:13–18).

The discourse on "the last things," which we find in Mark 13, owes much, as regards its form, to the fixed outline of early Christian preaching on the subject. Careful comparison with the Gospels of Matthew and Luke shows that sayings of Jesus, which were originally spoken at different times and places, have here been brought together into a connected discourse, in order to give to the church a word of comfort in relation to these "last things." It is in this sense that the chapter is to be understood. But what is contained in it has not been written in order to make it possible to calculate the exact date of the end of the world: "But of that day or that hour no one knows, not even the angels in heaven, nor the Son, but only the Father" (13:32). Any attempt at calculation is thus forbidden. The words which are spoken concerning the last things are spoken as a warning against being led astray (13:5, 23). According to God's secret counsel, a number of terrible events must happen one after the other (13:7). But God will stand by his own (13:11), and for their sakes will shorten the time of suffering, in order that they may be able to endure the trial (13:20).

As a warning, and as a consolation to the faithful, a picture is here built up which in its details is certainly terrifying. Prophecies which have to do with the destruction of the temple and of the holy city (13:1–2) are mixed up in strange fashion with others that look forward to the end of the world. Deceivers will appear; wars and rumors of war will spread; one people will rise up against another; earthquakes and famines will take place. But that is only the beginning of birth-pangs (13:5–8). Just as, once the birth-pangs have begun, the birth will certainly follow, so that which follows on this beginning will certainly come, and no one can change anything in it. The disciples of Jesus will be persecuted and brought to judgment; the father will betray the child, and the children their parents (13:9–13). But when the desolating sacrilege is set up where it ought not to be (i.e., in the temple), then the final misery has arrived. This is a reference in hidden terms to the antichrist (see Daniel 9:27; 11:31; 12:11). He who is in Judea should then flee without delay to the mountains—a prophecy which was fulfilled in the days of the war between the Jews and the Romans. These days will be so terrible that even the elect would not be able to endure them, unless the Lord had shortened the days. When distress, and the deception brought about by false prophets and false messiahs, have reached their climax (13:14–22), then "the sun will be darkened, and the moon will not give its light, and the stars will be falling from heaven, and the powers in the heavens will be shaken. And then they will see the Son of man coming in clouds with great power and glory" (13:24–27). Then the hour of deliverance is near. But when will this take place? No man knows the hour; but Jesus says: "What I say to you I say to all: Watch" (13:37). Watch—that is the command given to the fellowship of those who believe in Jesus Christ in the last days. For we do not know *when* the Lord will come, but we do know that he will come. Therefore, watch!

Here Mark brings to an end his account of the ministry and preaching of Jesus in Jerusalem. Immediately upon this follows the story of the passion. Does the career of Jesus end in catastrophe on the cross? From Chapter 13, the reader learns that the career of Jesus did not end on the cross, but that the crucified and risen Jesus is also the Lord who is to come, who will appear as the deliverer of his people, and as the judge of the living and the dead.

Thus this chapter also is part of the good news, bringing to the disciples of Jesus strength and encouragement "to wait for his Son from heaven, whom he raised from the dead, Jesus who delivers us from the wrath to come" (1 Thessalonians 1:10).

chapter 6

The Passion and Resurrection of Jesus Christ

JESUS CHRIST, the crucified and risen Messiah—this is the sum and substance of early Christian preaching. For the Evangelists, also, the crucial point of their story was necessarily the account of the cross and of the resurrection of Jesus Christ. That which in the proclamation of the church had been dealt with in brief phrases—Jesus Christ died for our sins according to the Scriptures—must here be set out at greater length in the narratives of the passion.

Certainly some of the stories which we find as parts of the passion-narrative, as we have it in Mark's Gospel, had circulated earlier in the oral tradition of the church as separate incidents. This is probably true of the story of the anointing of Jesus in 14:3–9; since we find Luke has no story of an anointing as part of his passion-narrative, but has such a story much earlier in his Gospel (Luke 7:36–50). Since the anointing was regarded as a preparation for the death and burial of Jesus, it was natural that this story should be brought into close relationship to the passion-narrative. Or again, we see from the account of the Last Supper which Paul gives to the Corinthians (1 Corinthians 11:23–26) that it was possible to speak of this event without giving at the same time a complete account of the passion. In order to understand this section, all that it was necessary for the reader to know was that the Lord Jesus, on the night in which he was betrayed and given up into the hands of men, had eaten and drunk with his disciples (14:18, 22–25). From such observations we may conclude that what we have in the account of the death and resurrection of Jesus Christ is not a formal and systematic account. What we here learn of the sufferings of Jesus has grown up from the living witness of faith, has been constantly repeated in the preaching of the church, and is now written in order to pass on to the reader the good news of the death of Christ, which he endured for our sakes. Of these events we have no neutral account, like the formal account of a trial. We have only a witness from faith to faith.

The early Christian preaching affirmed that Jesus had suffered, died, and risen again "according to the Scriptures." By this it was intended to make clear that his death was not something that happened by chance, that it was not a victory of his enemies or the tragic end of a great man. On the contrary, his death took place in obedience to the will of God—God had made his will known in advance, in the Scriptures of the Old Testament. But it was only through faith in Jesus Christ that the key had been given for a right understanding of those Scriptures (see Luke 24:13–35). Now for the first time it was possible to recognize in the Old Covenant that which had been written and spoken as a promise of the coming of the Christ. It was for this reason that the death of Jesus was understood as a fulfillment of the Scriptures. The story of the passion in Mark's Gospel is to be read in this sense. Jesus suffers and dies in order that the Scriptures may be fulfilled (14:49). In Mark's account of the passion there are only a few quotations from the Old Testament which are clearly indicated as such. But close study makes clear that at every point of the story, phrases from the Psalms and the prophets are introduced, and these indicate that at these points the Scriptures are in process of being fulfilled. In the following passages it is clear that these are allusions to something that has been foretold in the Old Testament:

Mark 14:18

"Truly, I say to you, one of you will betray me, one who is eating with me."

Psalm 41:9

"Even my bosom friend in whom I trusted,
who ate of my bread, has lifted his heel against me."

Mark 14:27

"You will all fall away; for it is written, 'I will strike the shepherd, and the sheep will be scattered.' "
(*This is an almost exact quotation from* Zechariah 13:7)

Mark 14:34

"My soul is very sorrowful, even to death."

Psalm 42:6, 11

"My soul is cast down within me."
"Why are you cast down, O my soul,
and why are you disquieted within me?"

Mark 14:57

"And some stood up and bore false witness against him."

Psalm 27:12

"Give me not up to the will of my adversaries;
for false witnesses have risen against me,
and they breathe out violence."

Mark 14:61; 15:5

(*Jesus is silent and answers nothing.*)

Isaiah 53:7

"He was oppressed, and he was afflicted,
yet he opened not his mouth;
like a lamb that is led to the slaughter,
and like a sheep that before its shearers is dumb,
so he opened not his mouth."

Mark 15:24

"They . . . divided his garments among them, casting lots for them, to decide what each should take."

Psalm 22:18

"They divide my garments among them,
and for my raiment they cast lots."

Mark 15:27

"With him they crucified two robbers, one on his right and one on his left."

Isaiah 53:12

"He . . . was numbered with the transgressors."

Mark 15:29–32

(*Jesus is mocked by those who pass by.*)

Psalm 22:7

"All who see me mock at me,
they make mouths at me, they wag their heads."

Mark 15:34

"Jesus cried with a loud voice, 'Eloi, Eloi, lama sabachthani?' which means 'My God, my God, why hast thou forsaken me?' "

(*An exact quotation from* Psalm 22:1.)

Mark 15:36

"And one ran and, filling a sponge full of vinegar, put it on a reed and gave it to him to drink."

Psalm 69:21

". . . and for my thirst they gave me vinegar to drink."

It was in the light of the Old Testament chapters from which these passages are quoted that the first Christians came to understand that the death of Jesus had taken place according to the will of God; in their accounts of the passion they gave expression to this understanding.

Mark's narrative of the passion opens with a decision of the chief priests and scribes to take Jesus secretly and to put him to death (14:1–2). Nothing could have been more convenient to them for the carrying out of their design than the help of Judas. For what Judas betrayed certainly included information as to the place in which Jesus was to be found. He told them where the Master would spend the night, so that they might capture him quietly and without making a disturbance. Of the reasons and motives which led Judas to betray his Master, we are told nothing. But the reader of the Gospel is not unprepared for this terrible deed, since in 3:19, Mark has already referred to Judas as the traitor. When Jesus tells the disciples that one of them will betray him and deliver him up, they are all horrified and say: "Lord, is it I?" It is intended that every disciple of Jesus should test himself with these words, in order to see whether it may not be he who is betraying his Master by what he does.

In Mark's account, the announcement of the betrayal takes place during the Last Supper, which Jesus took with his disciples. Mark records that this took place on the day of the feast of the Passover. Jesus and his disciples had come up to Jerusalem among the great crowd of pilgrims who were going up to keep the great feast in the holy city. Only within its walls could the festival be observed. Therefore, all Jews who wished to take part in it had to set forth and make their way to Jerusalem. The number of pilgrims was often larger than that of the inhabitants of the city. But for every citizen of Jerusalem it was a solemn duty to show hospitality to pious visitors.

Thus it came about that Jesus with his friends was able to find a place in which to keep the feast. In the days of the Passover all Israel recalled God's great act of deliverance, through which he had once brought the people out of their captivity in Egypt (Exodus 12—13). In memory of this event the paschal lambs were slain, and eaten at the sacred meal; the story of the Exodus was read, and Psalms of praise to God (113—118) were sung. The story of the Last Supper of Jesus with his disciples is fitted into this setting of the Passover story, through which its significance is made plain as one of God's historic acts of salvation. The first deliverance of Israel and the new deliverance in the end of the days are set side by side and in contrast to one another. Over against the covenant, which God made with Israel in the wilderness, is set the New Covenant, the new order, which is founded on the death of Jesus.

Jesus and his disciples eat together, as they had so often done during the lifetime of their Master (cf. 6: 34–44). Jesus, as the head of the family, takes the bread, pronounces the blessing, breaks it, and distributes it. In this way everyone who is present at the meal shares in the blessing which has been pronounced over it. Later, Jesus takes the cup, again pronounces a blessing, and gives it to the disciples to drink. Once again each receives his share of the blessing that has been uttered. What is the meaning of this solemnity? It is the last meal of Jesus with his friends. But what broods over it is not the sorrow of parting, but the triumph of the Messiah, who will come in his glory (14:25). The disciples will be left without him. But during this time, in which they will be left alone, Jesus assures them that he will be with them in the celebration of this meal. The blessing which he has pronounced over it makes plain to them its meaning. "Take, eat: this is my body." So Jesus had spoken of the bread. "I am this bread." Jesus is the bread of life, by which His Church lives. "This is my blood, which is shed for many." The new order of God is based on the death of Jesus. This covenant is ratified, not like the covenant of Sinai by animal sacrifices (Exodus 24:8), but by the death of the Servant of the Lord on behalf of men. This is the covenant of forgiveness, which the prophet had foretold for the latter days: "Behold the days are coming, says the Lord, when I will make a new covenant with the house of Israel. . . . I will put my law within them, and I will write it upon their hearts; and I will be their God, and they shall be my people. . . . for I will forgive their iniquity, and I will remember their sin no more" (Jeremiah 31:31–34). This has now become a present reality, since Jesus has died on behalf of many (see Leviticus 17:11–14). And here, as also in 10:45, "many" means "on behalf of all men." The Christ is not only the Messiah of Israel; he gives his life for all men and for all peoples. In their stead, he takes upon himself the destiny of death, in order that they may all live in God's new order and receive the forgiveness of their sins. These words, which announce the part which the death of Jesus will play in winning salvation for men, determine the meaning of the Last Supper. Whenever the disciples meet to observe the Supper, they will be partakers in the reconciling power of the death of Jesus, and will have fellowship with their exalted Lord.

The scene in the garden of Gethsemane shows us Jesus wrestling with the agony of temptation. At the beginning of his career (1:12 ff.), again in the words of Peter after the first prediction of His sufferings (8:32 ff.), and now once more, as he draws near to his cross, the tempter approaches, to draw him away from his obedience and his willingness to suffer. But Jesus overcomes the temptation through committing everything confidently into the hands of his heavenly Father. The story of the battle of Jesus with temptation is told simply and with restraint. We are forbidden to look deeply into his inner life; he stands before us simply as the Son who is obedient to his Father's will. Thus he shows his disciples how they too can overcome the temptation of the last time of suffering—in watchfulness and prayer to God as their Father (14:36–38).

Jesus is taken prisoner, and brought before the Sanhedrin. All the disciples forsake him and flee; even Peter denies his Lord. In the trial before the Sanhedrin, the highest authority of the Jews, it is revealed who Jesus is. The evidence of the witnesses draws attention to something that Jesus is alleged to have said: he would destroy the temple, and raise it up again in three days. It is only in the Fourth Gospel that we find this saying as actually uttered by Jesus (John 2:19–22). But it is evident that the point of this accusation against Jesus is its relation to his claim to be the Messiah. The high priest, who is presiding over the Sanhedrin, puts to Jesus directly the decisive question: "Are you the Christ, the Son of the Blessed?" (14:61). It was a part of the tradition of the Jews, from motives of reverence, never to pronounce the name of God; hence God is here referred to as "the Blessed." To this question Jesus answers "Yes"; full of majesty, he stands before his judges and affirms: "I am; and you will see the Son of man sitting at the right hand of Power [i.e., of God] and coming with the clouds of heaven." This is the climax of Mark's narrative of the passion. Jesus is the Messiah; in spite of all opposition, in the end his glory will be manifest.

At that time, the Jews were subject to the supreme authority of the Romans. Judea was governed by a Roman "procurator." The Roman Government had taken from the Jews the right to condemn a man to death and to carry out the sentence. This right was reserved to the Roman governor and to him alone. The Jews had, therefore, to deliver up to the Roman authority any man whom they regarded as worthy of death. What, then, would be the result of the trial of Jesus? According to Mark's account, the question of the Messiahship of Jesus was raised also in the trial before Pilate (15:1–5). A Messiah of the Jews might easily provoke a rebellion against the Romans. It was, therefore, very much to the interest of the Romans to put such dangerous people out of the way. Pilate, however, recognizes quite clearly that this prophet from Nazareth is not a political agitator. And yet to carry out this particular desire of the Jews, and in this point at least not to disappoint them, Pilate pronounces the sentence of condemnation.

Jesus is led out to be crucified outside the gates of Jerusalem. Whereas the Jews, following the rules of the Old Testament, carried out executions by stoning, the Romans crucified rebels, criminals, and slaves. This was the most terrible way of putting a man to death, since the victim often died miserably after endless sufferings. Jesus endured this shameful death.

On the way to the place of crucifixion Jesus broke down under the weight of the cross. The soldiers compelled a man who was passing by to take up the cross of Jesus and to carry it to the hill on which the execution was to take place. His name is given by Mark as Simon of Cyrene, the father of Alexander and Rufus. Now we learn from the Epistle of Paul to the Romans (Romans 16:13) that a man named Rufus and his mother were members of the Church of Rome. Clearly the purpose of Mark in mentioning this name was to make it clear that it was this Simon, the father of Rufus, who had been an eyewitness of the crucifixion of Jesus. He and his sons were well known in the Church for which Mark wrote his Gospel. This little detail of the story of the passion renders it probable that the Christians in Rome were the first readers of the Gospel according to St. Mark.

Mocked and reviled, alone and abandoned, Jesus hung upon the cross. Shortly before the end he cried out in the words of Psalm 22:1 "My God, my God, why hast thou forsaken me?" Is this cry that God had forsaken him a cry of despair? The words give evidence of the depth of the conflict and of the temptation that Jesus endured. Yet, for all that, it is a word of Scripture that he uses as a prayer; in his deepest need he still calls upon God as his God; the Son is still obedient to the Father. The cry of Jesus is thus not an expression of utter despair, but of obedient confidence in God. With a loud cry he breathes his last. Since men who had been crucified usually died slowly and miserably, whereas Jesus dies after only a few hours, and breathes his last with a loud cry, a special significance has sometimes been ascribed to this last cry of Jesus: he dies of his own free will; the Son of man is *giving* his life as a ransom for many.

The first man to confess faith in the crucified Christ was a heathen soldier, who had seen everything that had happened. "Truly this man was a son of God!" (15:39). The Son of God dies, he hangs on the cross: "Thou art my beloved Son; with thee I am well pleased" (1:11).

Jesus is buried; a stone is rolled before the entrance to his grave. On the third day, however, the day after the Sabbath—so it runs in Mark's account—women came to the grave in order to anoint the body (16:1–8). But they find the stone rolled back from the entrance to the tomb, and receive from the lips of an angel the news: "He has risen." Jesus is not among the dead; he is not here. Trembling and astonishment come upon the women. This is the awe which falls upon those who are brought into contact with the direct action of God. "They were afraid."

With these words ends the account given by Mark,* as it has come down to us. He lets us see clearly that he knows of other appearances of the risen Christ to his disciples (14:28; 16:7). The early Christian preaching particularly mentioned Peter and the Twelve as among those who had seen the risen Lord (1 Corinthians 15:5). But Mark gives us nothing but the information: "He has risen." Jesus has risen, and so God's new world has come into being. He is the Lord. In these words is included

---

* *Editorial Note on the end of St. Mark's Gospel:*

In the Authorized Version of the New Testament, Chapter 16 of the Gospel contains twenty verses. In the Revised Standard Version, only eight verses are printed in the text, and verses 9 to 20, and another shorter ending to the Gospel, are printed in smaller type in a note.

The reason for this change is that the old manuscripts of the Gospel in Greek and other ancient languages do not all give us the same evidence.

In the two oldest and best complete Greek manuscripts of the New Testament, we find only verses 1 to 8 of this chapter, and nothing after them.

In two old and important Greek manuscripts and some other sources, we find the second and shorter ending given in the Revised Standard Version.

In many later manuscripts we find verses 9 to 20.

Both these endings are very different in style from the rest of the Gospel, and it is certain that they are not part of what St. Mark wrote.

Some scholars think that the Gospel was intended to finish with verse 8, and that we have all that St. Mark wrote. Others think that St. Mark wrote a fuller account of the resurrection, but that what followed verse 8 has been lost. The last page of St. Mark's manuscript may have been torn off or otherwise accidentally lost. (This could easily happen in the days before printing, when all books existed only in manuscript.) Later, but still at a very early date, reverent readers of the Gospel, feeling that it was incomplete, added these various endings to round off the Gospel and to give it a completeness which they felt it lacked in the text as they had it before them.

everything that is essential to the faith of a Christian in his Lord. Perhaps it was the intention of Mark to limit the information he gives us about the resurrection of Jesus to these few brief words. No man can describe the process of the resurrection. No one can venture to say exactly what happened. Fear is the first reaction of men. Only later can the cry of joy break forth: "Christ is risen; he is risen indeed."

We do not know why Mark ended his narrative at this point. It is, of course, possible that the last section of his book has been lost. Matthew and Luke, who both knew and used the Gospel of Mark, were certainly acquainted with his narrative only up to this point, since it is only up to this point that Mark has served as the basis for what those two Gospels have in common. It was not long before it was felt as a defect that in Mark's Gospel there was only such a very brief account of the resurrection of Jesus. For this reason, in the second century A.D., Mark's account was completed by the addition of 16:9–20. This section presupposes that all four Gospels were available in their completed form; since it refers explicitly to several of the Easter stories in the other Gospels, and weaves them together into a harmony of the Gospels. We may note the following parallels: 16:9–11—John 20:11–18; 16:12–13—Luke 24:13–35; 16:14–16—Matthew 28:16–20; 16:19—Luke 24:50–53. This collection of passages is intended to make clear that the exalted Lord is always present in His Church, and gives power to the words of his witnesses (16:20).

The Gospel of Jesus Christ—that is, the proclamation of Jesus Christ as the crucified and risen Messiah. Mark sets forth this proclamation by collecting and writing the stories which tell of Jesus Christ as the Lord. Jesus of Nazareth is the Son of God. Through his deeds and words he manifested his glory. But only those who believe in him are able to recognize who he is. Mark was not himself a witness of the events which he describes. He has believed the testimony of the apostles and messengers. This message he wishes to pass on, in order that it may be received in faith. So of Mark's Gospel, as of the other Gospels, what John wrote about his own book is true: "These are written that you may believe that Jesus is the Christ, the Son of God, and that believing you may have life in his name" (John 20:31).